W9-BQT-189

# The New York Times

## CUP OF CROSSWORDS
### 75 Easy-to-Medium Crossword Puzzles

## Edited by Will Shortz

ST. MARTIN'S GRIFFIN ❧ NEW YORK

THE NEW YORK TIMES CUP OF CROSSWORDS.
Copyright © 2005 by The New York Times Company. All rights reserved.
Printed in the United States of America. No part of this book may be
used or reproduced in any manner whatsoever without written
permission except in the case of brief quotations embodied
in critical articles or reviews. For information, address
St. Martin's Press, 175 Fifth Avenue, New York, N.Y. 10010.

www.stmartins.com

All of the puzzles that appear in this work were originally published
in *The New York Times* from March 5, 2002, to August 26, 2002.
Copyright © 2002 by The New York Times Company.
All rights reserved. Reprinted by permission.

ISBN 0-312-33955-0
EAN 978-0312-33955-5

10  9  8  7  6  5  4  3  2

# The New York Times

## CUP OF CROSSWORDS

## ACROSS

1 Nav. officers
5 Muscle contraction
10 Madcap
14 Con ___ (vigorously)
15 Name tag word
16 Soothing plant extract
17 China/Korea border river
18 Disney's ___ Center
19 Church seating
20 Brainy
23 Kind of orange
24 Tex-Mex restaurant dip
28 Surgery locales: Abbr.
29 Gridiron great Groza
31 "You've got mail" co.
32 Words from Caesar
35 "Beyond Good and Evil" author
38 Brainy
41 Egotistical
42 Mindless repetition
43 Biblical verb ending
44 Attorneys' org.
45 Bring to bear
47 Coup ___
49 Symbol of Americanism
54 Brainy
57 Guitarist Hendrix
60 "Secrets & Lies" director Mike
61 Roman 152
62 Vicinity
63 "Exodus" actor Sal
64 "___ in Full" (Tom Wolfe novel)
65 Succotash tidbit
66 Uneasy feeling
67 Summoned help, maybe

## DOWN

1 Vast gulf
2 "Law & Order," e.g.
3 Where to see "The Last Supper"
4 San Francisco bread
5 Clippers
6 Coke competitor
7 Highway to Fairbanks
8 Gradual
9 Sweater eater
10 Inventor of the Mothers of Invention
11 Ginger ___
12 Right away
13 "You bet!"
21 Roofer's supply
22 Rodeo producer
25 Milk: Prefix
26 Not ___ (mediocre)
27 Coeur d'___, Idaho
29 One of two ballroom dancers
30 Horse picker's hangout, for short
32 Flowed back
33 Clichéd
34 Too snug
35 Zip, to Zapata
36 Suffix with expert
37 San Francisco transport
39 Shrubby land
40 Keyboard key
45 Outcome
46 Patty Hearst's kidnap grp. _IRA_
48 From the Orient
49 Imitating
50 Buzzes, say
51 Director Brian De ___
52 Suffix with beaut-
53 Stretching (out)
55 ___ mater
56 Jockey strap
57 Abrupt thrust
58 Wrath
59 ___ culpa

*by Marjorie Richter*

Grid fill:
- 1A: DMS
- 5A: SPASM
- 10A: ANY
- 14A: RIO
- 15A: HELLO
- 16A: ALOE
- 17A: YALU
- 18A: EPCOT
- 19A: PEWS
- 20A: SMARTASAWHIZ
- 23A: MANDARIN
- 24A: SALSA
- 28A: ORS
- 29A: LOU
- 31A: AOL
- 32A: ETTU
- 35A: NIETZSCHE
- 38A: BRIGHTASABUTTON
- 41A: BIGHEADED
- 42A: ROTE
- 43A: ETH
- 44A: ABA
- 47A: DETAT
- 49A: SHARPASATACK
- 57A: JIMI
- 60A: LEIGH
- 61A: CLII
- 62A: AREA
- 63A: MINEO
- 64A: MAN
- 65A: BEAN
- 66A: ANGST
- 67A: SOS

# 2

## ACROSS

1 90 degrees
5 Place for a cypress
10 Attempt
14 Be a monarch
15 Staples Center player
16 Hack
17 "Magnet and Steel" singer Walter
18 Word to a knight
19 Aspirin, e.g.
20 Reduce one's feelings of weariness?
23 Check for fit
24 Looped handle
25 Actress Campbell
28 Heavenly edible
33 Court decision
36 Play baseball with cheeses?
40 Water color
42 Seafood entree
43 Perplexity
44 Badly bruised president?
47 Rock producer Brian
48 Kind of bean
49 Over
51 Dutch export
55 Canadian peninsula
59 Master at wielding a tongue depressor?
64 Monopoly square
65 Piano specialist
66 Cut, as film
67 Pac 10 school
68 Grimalkin
69 Steam up
70 Keep at it
71 King of Judea
72 Sibyl

## DOWN

1 Be constructive?
2 Foreshadow
3 Dark bluish-gray
4 Muscle/bone connector
5 Common side order
6 Put on notice
7 Japanese dog
8 Elementary particle
9 Urge
10 Dateless
11 Dial on the dash
12 Central line
13 Didn't pass
21 First-floor apartment
22 Shakespeare's foot?
26 Bud holder
27 Make an artistic impression
29 Famous holder of pairs
30 1982 Tony musical
31 Broadway brightener
32 Regarding
33 Arctic native
34 Prefix akin to iso-
35 Change colors
37 Singing syllable
38 Georgetown athlete
39 Adam's apple area?
41 Fitting
45 MGM Studios founder
46 Utah's state flower
50 Thin treats
52 Get rid of
53 Lapis lazuli
54 House of lords
56 "Sexy" Beatles girl
57 Audio attachment?
58 Any acetate, chemically
59 Food whose name means, literally, wadding
60 Hawaiian port
61 Zing
62 Attorney general from Miami
63 Stowe book
64 Water carrier

*by Richard Silvestri*

## ACROSS

**1** Sixth Greek letter
**5** Short hit, in baseball
**9** Specialized vocabulary
**14** Tennis great Lendl
**15** "___ bitten, twice shy"
**16** Crystal-lined stone
**17** Barbershop call
**18** Place for "junk"
**20** Emergency situation that an Egyptian goddess experiences?
**22** Spell-off
**23** Golf ball peg
**24** Down's opposite
**28** ___ and aahs
**30** Head-butt
**33** Three-wheeler
**34** Thin wedge of wood
**35** Stew holders
**36** Fruit that grandma dubbed?
**39** Rooney of "60 Minutes"
**40** Place to stroll
**41** Refrain in "Old MacDonald"
**42** Magic 8-Ball answer
**43** Sherlock Holmes prop
**44** Beauty parlors
**45** "Thar ___ blows!"
**46** Permit
**47** Ornate clone of designer Chanel?
**55** Big political contest
**56** Buckeye's home
**57** Foreword, for short
**58** Slender nail
**59** Child with no siblings
**60** Parts of houses and mouths
**61** Shopper stopper
**62** ___ pony

## DOWN

**1** Metal in brass
**2** ". . . happily ___ after"
**3** Way around town
**4** Aardvark's fare
**5** Supervisors
**6** Loosen, as laces
**7** Sgts. and cpls.
**8** Actress Hatcher
**9** Texas A&M's team
**10** Baseball great Pee Wee
**11** Mongolian desert
**12** Scandinavian god
**13** Royal flush card
**19** Breathing woe
**21** "A Doll's House" playwright
**24** Unable to flee
**25** Origami bird
**26** Orange covers
**27** Approve
**28** Chicago airport
**29** Sound in "Old MacDonald"
**30** One of Shakespeare's "star-crossed lovers"
**31** Didn't go out to a restaurant
**32** Forerunner of Windows
**34** Rice Krispies sound
**35** Bucket
**37** Each
**38** "Cool!"
**43** Wedding album contents
**44** Withdraw (from)
**45** Winter wear
**46** Making all stops
**47** Nevada city
**48** "I'm ___ you!"
**49** Spheres
**50** Singer Irene
**51** Condo's cousin
**52** Speed skater Apolo Anton ___
**53** Tablet
**54** It has its ups and downs
**55** Knight's title

| Z | E | T | A | | B | U | N | T | | A | G | T | A |
| I | V | A | N | | O | N | C | E | | G | E | O | C |
| N | E | X | T | | S | T | O | R | A | G | E | B | E |
| C | R | I | S | I | S | I | S | I | S | I | | I | R |
| | | | B | E | E | | | T | E | E | | | |
| A | C | R | O | S | S | | O | O | H | S | | R | A | M |
| T | R | I | K | E | | S | H | I | M | | P | O | T | S |
| B | A | N | A | N | A | N | A | N | A | N | A | M | E | D |
| A | N | D | Y | | P | A | R | K | | E | I | E | I | O |
| Y | E | S | | P | I | P | E | | S | A | L | O | N | S |
| | | | S | H | E | | L | E | T | | | | |
| R | I | C | O | C | O | C | O | C | O | | O | P | |
| S | E | N | A | T | E | R | A | C | E | | O | H | I | O |
| I | N | T | R | O | | B | R | A | D | | O | N | L | Y |
| R | O | O | F | S | | S | A | L | E | | O | L | |

*by Peter Gordon*

**4**

## ACROSS

1 Artist Chagall
5 Rams' mates
9 Hairy-chested ones
14 Former Expos manager Felipe
15 À la mode
16 Use a soapbox
17 Scorch
18 Frequent quarreler with Zeus
19 Chop finely
20 Oil container #1
23 On the briny
24 Melody
25 ___-de-France
28 Oil container #2
33 Neighbor of Syr.
36 Downfall
37 Pitcher Ryan
38 "The Intimate ___" (1990 jazz album)
40 Disgusted
43 Capone's nemesis
44 English actors Bates and Rickman
46 Granola bits
48 Play thing
49 Oil container #3
53 "Naughty!"
54 Many a crossword clue
55 Follow
59 Oil container #4
64 Novel or essay
66 Desert bordered by steppe land
67 French cleric
68 "The House of the Seven Gables" locale
69 Place for a spending spree
70 Apple throwaway

71 Nobel, for one
72 One way to orient a boat
73 Greek H's

## DOWN

1 Tuscan city noted for its marble quarries
2 Alaskan native
3 Dappled horses
4 A time to remember?
5 Reverberate
6 "That was a close one!"
7 Leprechaun's land
8 Sacred beetle
9 Big hit
10 Enemies of the Iroquois
11 Lower jaws

12 Often-repeated abbr.
13 Maiden name preceder
21 Bert of "The Wizard of Oz"
22 The "S" in R.S.V.P.
26 Rent
27 Young's partner in accounting
29 ___ Wiedersehen
30 Tell tall tales
31 At the ___ one's rope
32 "___ voyage!"
33 Vaulted
34 "Less Than Zero" novelist
35 Very attractive body?
39 Queen's subject, possibly

41 Old Mideast inits.
42 "Harper Valley ___"
45 Above all others
47 "Peter Pan" character
50 Capek play
51 Riddle
52 Unite threads
56 Wooden shoe
57 Planetary shadow
58 Fencing needs
60 Secondhand
61 Brat's stocking stuffer
62 Highly adroit
63 Blue or White follower
64 Supp. writings
65 Untreated

*by Sarah Keller*

## ACROSS

1 Black Caucus, e.g.
5 Borscht makings
10 Prefix with carpal
14 1972 Kentucky Derby winner ___ Ridge
15 More than fancy
16 Mysterious byline, for short
17 Start of a cynic's definition of "love"
19 Burglar
20 "Oh, Lady, Be Good" writer
21 Reef material
22 Lunch hour, maybe
23 With 43-Down, author of the definition
25 Vamooses
29 Causes gasps
30 Skin flicks
31 Put ___ appearance
32 Kind of spirit
36 Middle of the definition
39 Element #10
40 New Mexico resort
41 Cheeses in red wax
42 Ego
43 Safari chiefs
44 Private school
48 Cousin of "Ugh!"
49 Congo Basin river
50 Pink-flowered shrub
55 Proctor's announcement
56 End of the definition
58 Paleozoic and Cenozoic
59 Hyperactive
60 Like a beanpole
61 Tent furniture
62 Indefinite wait
63 "What ___ could I do?"

## DOWN

1 Crow
2 For the calorie-conscious
3 In excess of
4 Engine parts
5 Seven-time N.F.L. East champions in the 1950's
6 Spooky
7 Cardinal O'Connor's successor
8 Cigarette stat
9 Winking, maybe
10 1984 Ed Koch best seller
11 Año starter
12 "Animal House" party wear
13 Turn sharply
18 Massless particle
21 Dan Rather's employer
23 Radar-equipped plane
24 Waiter's offering
25 Test drive
26 Christmas decoration
27 Guess qualifier
28 Son of Judah
29 "Don't give me ___ your lip!"
31 Part of a continental tour
32 Unveiler's cry
33 Abba of Israel
34 "Summer and Smoke" heroine
35 Word before call or hall
37 News bit
38 Don't change out of
42 Understand
43 See 23-Across
44 Montezuma, e.g.
45 Where "Aida" premiered
46 Shoot for
47 Toggery
48 Thrash
50 Old Dodge
51 Dark time, informally
52 Author Roald
53 Patronage: Var.
54 Actress Russo
56 Audi competitor
57 Derisive cry

*by Ed Early*

## ACROSS

1 Players in a play
5 Tobacco smoke component
8 Scottish Gaelic
12 Commedia dell'___
13 Visibly umbstruck
15 Trust, with "on"
16 Wheedle
17 Stick-on
18 Not fully closed
19 Puccini opera Web site?
22 Unlatch, to bards
23 Intl. cultural org.
24 Saigon's former enemy
26 60's campus grp.
27 Exact-time Web site?
32 "Don't go!"
33 Post-Crucifixion sculpture
34 Humid
38 Milky gems
41 Farmer's output
42 Violinist Stern
44 "Bye-bye"
46 Document miniaturization Web site?
49 Kwik-E-Mart clerk on "The Simpsons"
52 Where Goodyear is headquartered
53 Brunch dish
55 Tavern
57 Printed clothing Web site?
60 Elvis ___ Presley
62 Painter Rivera
63 Prefix with scope or logical
64 With 11-Down, Brontë heroine
65 Particle in electrolysis
66 R.&B. singer Redding
67 Reached ground
68 "___ Rosenkavalier"
69 Points per game, e.g.

## DOWN

1 It has points in Arizona
2 "I Get ___" (Beach Boys hit)
3 Rubbernecks
4 Lubbock's home
5 Discretion
6 Attack helicopter
7 Insert fresh cartridges
8 Silent ___ (time before the talkies)
9 Celebrant
10 Response to an affront
11 See 64-Across
13 Expand, as a house
14 Pres. Washington
20 Sgts. and such
21 Alphabet series
25 Suffix with psych-
28 Spigot
29 Marriott competitor
30 Great Plains Indian
31 Treasure hunter's aid
34 Slow-witted
35 "___ was saying"
36 Food that can be strung on a necklace
37 Driving test directive
39 Fond du ___, Wis.
40 Was atop
43 Company: Abbr.
45 Bullets
47 Thingamabob
48 Part of AOL
49 "Little Women" writer
50 Bradley University site
51 Maximum extent
54 Group's character
55 ___ California
56 Asia's ___ Sea
58 Actor Dullea
59 In times past
61 After-tax take

by John Greenman

## ACROSS

**1** Locker room handout
**6** Alma __
**11** Madison Avenue products
**14** Post of etiquette
**15** Line to the audience
**16** Dog doc
**17** News host, e.g.
**19** Gabor or Perón
**20** It may be bitter
**21** "Uh-uh"
**22** Token of respect
**24** Gossip's attribute
**28** Sandal feature
**30** Former partner?
**31** Sauce with basil
**32** Toast toppings
**33** Grub
**34** Part of LED
**36** Grub
**40** Whittle down
**41** Reporter's question
**42** Deejay's bribe
**45** 32-Across, e.g.
**47** Sign of unfaithfulness
**49** Angelic strings
**50** Long, long time
**51** Misfortune
**54** Simile's center
**55** Bit of aid
**59** Hamster, e.g.
**60** Bay window
**61** Bathed
**62** Wind dir.
**63** Aquarium favorite
**64** Poem of lament

## DOWN

**1** Head of France?
**2** Muscat's land
**3** Kind of show
**4** Lodge member
**5** Deceiving
**6** Noisy bird
**7** White-faced
**8** Haberdashery item
**9** Author LeShan
**10** Cinnamon treats
**11** Exact retribution for
**12** Gobble up
**13** Glassy look
**18** NASA scrub
**23** N.Y. neighbor
**25** Small colonists
**26** Garden bloom, informally
**27** Hardly racy
**28** Reveal, poetically
**29** Stew item
**32** __ Six-Pack
**34** Painter of limp watches
**35** Farsi-speaking land
**36** "Believe" singer
**37** Dog days phenomenon
**38** Former California fort
**39** Director Craven
**40** Aimless bit of gunfire
**41** Quarrel noisily
**42** Moon stages
**43** Make bubbly
**44** Big mouth
**45** Aussie lassie
**46** Lowly laborer
**47** Rodeo wear
**48** Slack-jawed one
**52** Force on earth, briefly
**53** MacDonald's partner in old movies
**56** Bard's before
**57** Inebriated
**58** "2001" computer

by Louis Hildebrand

(Completed grid)

- 1-Across: TOWEL
- 6-Across: MATER
- 11-Across: ADS
- 14-Across: EMILY
- 15-Across: ASIDE
- 16-Across: VET
- 17-Across: TALKINGHEAD
- 19-Across: EVA
- 20-Across: END
- 21-Across: NOPE
- 22-Across: HONOR
- 24-Across: WAGGINGTONGUE
- 28-Across: OPENTOE
- 30-Across: LATTER
- 31-Across: PESTO
- 32-Across: JAMS
- 33-Across: EATS
- 34-Across: DIODE
- 36-Across: CHOW
- 40-Across: PARE
- 41-Across: WHERE
- 42-Across: PAYOLA
- 45-Across: SPREADS
- 47-Across: CHEATINGHEART
- 49-Across: HARPS
- 50-Across: AEON
- 51-Across: WOE
- 54-Across: ASA
- 55-Across: HELPINGHAND
- 59-Across: PET
- 60-Across: ORIEL
- 61-Across: LAVED
- 62-Across: SSE
- 63-Across: TETRA
- 64-Across: ELEGY

# 8

## ACROSS

1 Walkers, for short
5 Leave untouched
10 Humorist Lebowitz
14 "Essays of __"
15 Maintains
16 Eastern music
17 Not lopsided
18 Nomination for which Susan Lucci finally won an Emmy
20 Setting for a shoot-'em-up
22 Expunge
23 Natl. Courtesy Mo.
24 As well
27 Dijon water
28 Black and white?
32 "Well!"
34 Ungracious winner
37 "How the Other Half Lives" author
38 2000 Mel Gibson flick
41 Svelte
42 About half of villagers
43 Virgil figure
46 Common plea, informally
47 One who's very wet?
50 Appt. calendar notation
51 New Deal org.
53 Contest effort
55 Surfers' place
59 High spirits
62 Prefix with byte
63 In a tizzy
64 Chicken parts

65 Earth sci.
66 Reasons
67 Salute, say
68 Jacket part

## DOWN

1 Midget
2 #1 Oak Ridge Boys hit
3 Split one's sides
4 Contents of hourglasses
5 Legal scholar Guinier
6 Axis of __
7 Care for
8 Pub orders
9 High regard
10 Guitarist's worry?
11 Campaigned
12 F.B.I. employee: Abbr.

13 "I don't think so"
19 Catch sight of
21 "__ the Beat" (Go-Go's hit)
24 Reconsiders
25 Leave out
26 Sounds of woe
29 Rarer than rare
30 Speck
31 Land on the Red Sea
33 Kind of agreement
35 Area between stripes
36 Get-hitched-quick spot
38 Sharpen
39 Gridiron org.
40 Went to court?
41 Pompom holder
44 Object of a manhunt, maybe

45 Leapt
48 The Snake borders it
49 Mercutio's killer, in "Romeo and Juliet"
52 Change
54 Israeli desert
55 Drag queen's collection
56 Chop up
57 Came alive
58 Part of N.I.H.: Abbr.
59 Talking point?
60 "Yuk!"
61 Lad

*by Elizabeth C. Gorski*

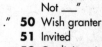

## ACROSS

1 Tail motions
5 Wheelchair-accessible route
9 Harvest
13 Needlecase
14 Braga from Brazil
15 "Cogito ___ sum"
16 Columnist Bombeck
17 Sweethearts of Sigma Chi
18 Losing effort?
19 Light modifiers
22 Utter
23 Big wine holder
24 Aussie hopper, for short
25 Goal
26 Leave earth?
31 Scarlett of Tara
34 Pharmacist's weight
35 "Get it?"
36 Temptations for spouses
40 Hawaiian wreath
41 "Put ___ on it!"
42 Some tests
43 Europe, Asia and Africa
46 Yea's opposite
47 Mich. neighbor
48 Brillo pad competitor
49 ___ Khan
52 Some thrown baseballs
57 Home run hitter Ruth
58 Surf sounds
59 "___ if you . . ." (bumper sticker)
60 Kiln
61 Feared eel
62 French friend
63 Dampens
64 Alteration canceler
65 Oboe, for one

## DOWN

1 Grass chokers
2 Skylit lobbies
3 Like envelope seals
4 Thailand, once
5 Night stick?
6 All over again
7 Skirt that goes below the knee
8 Deli meat on rye
9 Extremely popular
10 New York's ___ Canal
11 Many moons
12 Flower holder
14 "Git!"
20 Perrier rival
21 Businesses: Abbr.
25 "Roses ___ red . . ."
26 Hair feature
27 Fat
28 Govt. watchdog
29 Touch
30 Own (up to)
31 Norway's capital
32 Shoe part
33 Gung-ho
34 Wooded valley
37 Rigging supports
38 Words to a bride and groom
39 Have a bawl
44 Adds a lane to
45 Lonely number
46 Clamorous
48 Jack of nursery rhyme
49 "A House Is Not ___"
50 Wish granter
51 Invited
52 Goalie's action
53 "Oh, sure"
54 Cheer (for)
55 Stallion's mate
56 Blacken
57 Arrow shooter

*by Gerald R. Ferguson*

| W | A | G | S | | R | A | M | P | | R | E | A | P |
|---|---|---|---|---|---|---|---|---|---|---|---|---|---|
| E | T | U | I | | S | O | N | I | A | | E | R | G | O |
| F | R | M | A | | C | O | E | D | S | | D | I | E | T |
| D | I | M | M | E | R | S | W | I | T | C | H | E | S | |
| S | A | Y | | V | A | T | | | L | O | O | | | |
| | | | A | I | M | | B | L | A | S | T | O | F | F |
| O | H | A | R | A | | G | R | A | M | | S | E | E | |
| S | E | V | E | N | Y | E | A | R | I | T | C | H | E | S |
| L | E | I | | A | L | I | D | | O | R | A | L | S | |
| O | L | D | W | O | R | L | D | | N | A | V | | | |
| | | I | N | D | | S | O | S | | A | G | A | | |
| S | I | D | E | A | R | M | P | I | T | C | H | E | S | |
| B | A | B | E | | R | O | A | R | S | | H | O | N | K |
| O | V | E | N | | M | O | R | A | Y | | A | M | I | E |
| W | E | T | S | | S | T | E | T | | | R | E | E | D |

## ACROSS

1 Dogpatch cartoonist
5 Prefix with byte
9 Book after Hebrews
14 Away from the wind
15 "Oh dear!"
16 10% taker
17 Job enders
19 Dweebish
20 Christmas season
21 Singer DiFranco
23 Actor's prompt
24 Writer/director Nicholas
26 Tours within tours
29 G.P.'s grp.
30 Phaser setting
32 Go a-courting
33 Sound in the head
35 Concern of 41-Down: Abbr.
36 Stingless flier
39 Descending into ruin
43 Bruce of comedy
44 Singer Sumac
45 Chem. and bio.
46 Back on board
47 Kinks song of 1970
49 Newt
50 Malibu menaces
54 Some stereos
56 "Double Fantasy" musician
57 "What Kind of Fool __?"
58 Auctioneer's "Sold!"
59 "Hit the road!"
61 Idaho city
66 Crème de la crème
67 Scotch partner
68 Martinique et Guadeloupe
69 Splinter groups
70 "That hurts!"
71 Clancy hero Jack

## DOWN

1 Upper limit
2 Thrilla in Manila boxer
3 Small-time
4 Sri Lanka export
5 Shopaholic's heaven
6 Gin-maker Whitney
7 Clothing store, with "The"
8 Syrian president Bashar al-___
9 They have sweeping responsibilities
10 Secret stat, sometimes
11 French thanks
12 Eventually become
13 Eye sores
18 Sun. talks
22 F.D.R. program
24 Sitcom set in Korea
25 Messages via modem
26 Like anthems
27 Chic
28 Movable castles
31 Dickens boy
34 Old lab heaters
37 Bluenose
38 Instruct morally
40 One way to go down
41 Managed care grps.
42 Boom producers
48 Beginning on
50 He took two tablets
51 "That's enough!"
52 Classical column style
53 Addlebrained
55 Studio sign
58 Bite like a beaver
60 A.B.A. member: Abbr.
62 Misery
63 Promising words
64 Grazing locale
65 Tax form datum: Abbr.

*by Nancy Salomon and Harvey Estes*

## ACROSS

1 ___ Romeo
5 Prohibits
9 Feature of most roofs
14 Dappled horse
15 Shaving cream ingredient
16 Spud
17 Border upon
18 Getting warm, say
19 Unqualified
20 Winner of a belt
23 Furthermore
24 Long, long time
25 Easily provoked, as a temper
31 It stands at stands
34 Plead a case
35 Shed
36 Mystery writer Nevada
37 Animator's portfolio items
38 ___-ski
39 Concession closer?
40 Tie-up
41 Lyra's brightest star
42 Wall hanging
43 ___ Paulo
44 Ballpark figure?
46 Hula hoop?
47 Wore away
48 Fine flatware
56 Fleece
57 Potatoes partner
58 Slick
59 Costner's "Tin Cup" co-star
60 Far from ruddy
61 Snoop (around)
62 Bury

63 Sail support
64 Amber brews

## DOWN

1 Horse of the desert
2 Gray wolf
3 Not genuine, as gems
4 Like some business suits?
5 City on the Penobscot
6 One of the Baldwins
7 Ham's father
8 "Que" follower, in song
9 Daze
10 It can be vulgar
11 Conductor Klemperer
12 Ball-shaped hammer part
13 Goof
21 Word before a colon
22 Confronts
25 Penny-a-liners
26 Sports venue
27 Winter home, perhaps
28 Urge forward
29 Bungee jump site
30 Gather
31 So-called "City of Victory"
32 Pianist Claudio
33 French naval base
36 Where the Dream Team debuted
38 Benefit
42 Piedmont province
44 More than a brat

45 Oenologist, at times
46 Take temporarily
48 Never touch
49 Word after high or road
50 Little demons
51 Semimonthly tide
52 Big bash
53 Six-stringed instrument
54 Last word in an ultimatum
55 Some whiskeys
56 ___ Lanka

by Sarah Keller

| A | L | F | A |  | B | A | N | S |  | S | L | O | P | E |
| R | O | A | N |  | A | L | O | E |  | T | A | T | E | R |
| A | B | U | T |  | N | E | A | R |  | U | T | T | E | R |
| B | O | X | I | N | G | C | H | A | M | P | I | O | N |  |
|  |  |  |  |  |  |  |  | E | O | N |  |  |  |  |
|  |  |  |  |  |  |  |  | R |  |  |  |  |  |  |
|  |  | A | C |  |  |  |  |  |  |  |  |  |  |  |
|  |  | R | A |  |  |  |  |  |  | B |  |  |  |  |
|  |  | E | D |  |  |  |  |  |  | A |  |  |  |  |
|  |  | N | I |  |  |  |  |  |  | R |  |  |  |  |
| S | A | N |  |  | T |  |  |  |  | C |  |  |  |  |
|  |  |  |  | L | E | I |  |  |  |  |  |  |  |  |
| S | T | E | R | L | I | N | G | S | I | L | V | E | R |  |
| S | H | E | A | R |  |  | M | E | A | T |  | O | I | L | Y |
| R | U | S | S | O |  |  | P | A | L | E |  | N | O | S | E |
| I | N | T | E | R |  |  | S | T | A | Y |  | A | L | E | S |

# 12

## ACROSS

1 Scrounges (for)
6 Antlered animals
10 New Testament book
14 Move rapidly toward
15 Wordwise Webster
16 When doubled, quickly
17 ___ Sam
18 Dog in Oz
19 "___ Lee" (classic song)
20 Like some figures
22 Dad, slangily
24 Part of a process
25 Luau memento
26 Skater Babilonia
27 1986 sci-fi sequel
30 Fundamental
34 Free access
37 Third word in "America"
39 Pitcher's stat
40 See eye-to-eye?
44 Krazy ___
45 "Sprechen ___ Deutsch?"
46 Seas
47 Model's session
50 Like salmon, often
52 Certain retriever, briefly
54 Knock off, to a mobster
55 Statutes
59 Maine's ___ National Park
62 Stop signal
64 Buddy
65 Medical liquids
67 Playing marble
68 ___ Bora (Afghan region)
69 Numbered club
70 Part of an egg
71 Bridge
72 Train segments
73 Prepare, as tea

## DOWN

1 Beetle larvae
2 Charge
3 "I give!"
4 Shea, for one
5 Footfall
6 Meat dish, often
7 Examine oneself
8 Kit ___ bar
9 "Darn!"
10 "Evangeline" setting
11 Fish scraps
12 When tripled, a W.W. II movie
13 Nine inches
21 Ones with green cards
23 Igor's place
28 Hawaii's ___ Day
29 You: Ger.
31 "Will be," to Doris Day
32 Unwrinkle
33 "Shake It Up" band, with "the"
34 Fraternal members
35 Man famous for doing a double take?
36 In ___ (entirely)
38 Had Marlboros, say
41 Notes after las
42 "Rocks"
43 Kind of district
48 Hemingway title character
49 Mai ___
51 "___ Eleven" (Sinatra film)
53 Microsoft's first product
56 Texas A&M player
57 Like a surrender flag
58 Very expensive
59 Does stage work
60 Cut of lamb
61 Radiant glow
63 Samuel ___, inventor of the stock ticker
66 Paleozoic, for one

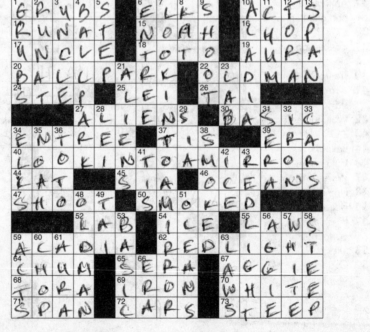

by Roger Barkan

# 13

## ACROSS

1 High land
5 Brewers' needs
9 Red Cross supplies
13 Spoken
14 Got close to
16 With 37- and 57-Across, a common warning
18 Taco holders
19 Sudden burst
20 Friend of Pooh
21 Six-pointers, for short
24 Cold war foe
25 Corn bread
28 Spy's device
31 Italian dramatist Pirandello
33 Prize that Pirandello won in 1934
34 Pitcher's asset
37 See 16-Across
40 Pilot's announcement, briefly
41 Haughty ones
42 Kind of blade
43 Cuff site
45 The Big Board: Abbr.
46 Choir member
49 WNW's opposite
50 Make stuff up
52 Bow parts
54 Present and future
57 See 16-Across
62 More than great
63 Covered
64 Sound of a leak
65 In __ (existing)
66 Bowlers and boaters

## DOWN

1 Swab
2 Memorable times
3 Obi
4 Mr. Hyde, to Dr. Jekyll
5 One of a pair of vanity plates
6 Not working
7 Favoring
8 "My dear man"
9 Take quickly
10 Ferber and others
11 Four-sided figs.
12 "Doe, __ . . ."
14 Not on deck
15 Dash lengths
17 Arafat's grp.
21 What ignoring this puzzle's warning may mean
22 Knock down
23 Suffix with young
25 Ballet bend
26 Depose
27 Ship of 1492
29 Gold bars
30 Winglike
32 Guy Lombardo's "__ Lonely Trail"
34 A.B.A. member: Abbr.
35 Classic cars
36 A __ child
38 Author Rice
39 Paragon
43 Easy outs
44 Unaccompanied part songs
46 At __ for words
47 Upper levels
48 Soy foods
51 Elected ones
53 Sault __ Marie
54 Align
55 Singer Fitzgerald
56 Urgent in the E.R.
58 French one
59 Hwys.
60 Goddess of the morning
61 1960's radical grp.

*by Janice M. Putney*

## 14

### ACROSS

1 ___ C. Dobbs, noted Humphrey Bogart role
5 Hearty cheers
9 More cheerful
14 Letterhead graphic
15 Turkish dough
16 "The Canterbury Tales" pilgrim
17 Brother of Little Joe
18 Dubya and classmates
19 Reo contemporary
20 Marxist patronage of the far left?
23 Trap
24 Apartment prohibition, maybe
28 Wrigley Field flora
29 Prohibitionist's foe
31 Quick trip
32 Dove's goal
35 Begot
37 "Am ___ believe . . . ?"
38 Marxist Muppet?
41 Sport ___ (modern vehicle)
42 They "all" have a day
43 Get-go
44 Snitched
46 McCarthy target
47 Much spam
48 Radioman's nickname
50 It may prove paternity
54 Marxist wind instrument?
57 Sound of an empty stomach
60 Sister of Charles and Andrew
61 Born's partner

62 "Jurassic Park" star Sam
63 Machu Picchu native
64 "Damn Yankees" vamp
65 ___-walsy
66 Season of giving
67 60's TV's ___ May Clampett

### DOWN

1 Boater's S O S
2 Tokyo trasher, in a 1956 film
3 "Good grief!"
4 West Indian nation
5 Fabled cow owner
6 De Gaulle's birthplace
7 Writer Hoffer
8 Merit badge spot

9 ___-Roman
10 "___ Fables"
11 "You bet!"
12 Early evictee
13 Mardi Gras figure
21 Spelunkers
22 Part of ICBM
25 "Cast-of-thousands" films
26 Tenth part
27 Uppity sort
29 Handle skillfully
30 Joule fractions
32 Broods
33 Bar, at the bar
34 Amtrak's bullet train
35 "Leaving Las Vegas" actress
36 Part of "De Camptown Races" refrain
39 Bit of statuary

40 Like nitroglycerin
45 Talks Dixie-style
47 Temper, as metal
49 Clown Emmett
50 Cut a rug
51 Flynn who played Robin Hood
52 Magic effect
53 Now
55 Reclined
56 ___ uncertain terms
57 Econ. measure
58 "Citizen X" actor, 1995
59 Wildcatter's find

by Fred Piscop

## ACROSS

1 Decoration on an Indian moccasin
5 Sound of astonishment
9 Relative of a croc
14 Therefore
15 Long (for)
16 Blazing
17 "You said it!"
18 Tall tale teller
19 Like property for businesses
20 "Good Will Hunting" actress
23 Beneath
24 Ferdinand's queen
28 Shooter pellet
29 Compete (for)
32 Storage places
33 Theater district
35 Helps out
36 St. Paul's twin
39 Kindergartners learn them
41 Competed at Henley
42 Least healthy
45 6-0 or 7-6, in tennis
46 Opponent
49 Nylon and others, chemically speaking
51 180° reversal
53 Electronic development of the 1960's
56 Thread holder
59 Mafia boss
60 Latvian capital
61 The "L" of AWOL
62 Choir voice
63 Sorry failure
64 "Holy cow!"
65 For fear that
66 Transmitted

## DOWN

1 Transport to the Enterprise, say
2 Luxury fur
3 "To do" list
4 "No man is an island" writer
5 Forceful wind
6 Citric ___
7 Puppeteer Lewis
8 U-boat features
9 Garden structure
10 Previously mentioned
11 & 12 Source of metal for cans
13 Scarlet
21 Rea ___, noted New Yorker cartoonist
22 Actor Kilmer
25 Oahu wreaths
26 Inc., abroad
27 Ninny
30 James Bond creator Fleming
31 Like house wiring
33 Double-crossing a Mafia boss, e.g.
34 Blacken
36 1250, in old Rome
37 Be indebted to
38 Abate
39 Nile biter
40 Life lines?
43 Writer Zola and others
44 Member of Cong.
46 Pointless
47 Salem's home
48 Transported
50 Climb
52 Home territories
54 Chooses
55 Not worth debating
56 Foxy
57 Rock and Roll Hall of Fame architect
58 Durable wood

by Richard Chisholm

# 16

## ACROSS
1 Impertinent talk
5 Shopaholic's binge
10 Pond organism
14 Taxing trip
15 Popular golf event
16 Satiric Sahl
17 Comrade in arms
18 Shred
19 Frankenstein's assistant
20 Source of sudden wealth
22 Dracula portrayer, 1931
24 "__ a traveler from an antique land": "Ozymandias"
25 Source of sudden wealth
26 Exceed
29 Central American Indians
30 Green Gables girl
31 Peter, pumpkinwise
32 Watchdog's warning
35 Possible title for this puzzle
39 Hosp. sections
40 Itsy-bitsy biters
41 "__ Was a Rollin' Stone"
42 Lip-__ (fakes singing)
43 Made use of
45 Source of sudden wealth
48 Drops from the sky
49 Newsman Peter
50 Source of sudden wealth
54 Feline line
55 Wrinkle removers
57 "Mm-hmm"
58 __ noire

59 Tropical fruit
60 It's the geologist's fault
61 Musher's transport
62 Incite
63 Young newts

## DOWN
1 All-male
2 Folk singer Guthrie
3 Pitch
4 High jumper?
5 Relatively agile
6 Word processor command
7 Hitchcock film
8 Vichy water
9 One on the payroll
10 Guadalajara girlfriends
11 Access the Web
12 100th of a zloty
13 Skylit lobbies
21 Marseille Mrs.
23 Take a revolver from
25 Bubbling waters
26 Marvin of Motown
27 __ about (roughly)
28 Burden
29 Damon and Lauer
31 Put on the books
32 Nibble away
33 Seized vehicle
34 "Saving Private __"
36 Pharaoh's land
37 Lickety-split
38 "Shoot!"
42 Distorted
43 "Cheers" star
44 Purge
45 Doorway sides
46 Staggering
47 100 smackers
48 Fab Four drummer
50 "The World of Suzie __" (1960 movie)
51 "Like, no way!"
52 Took a powder
53 Polite response to an invitation
56 Unprestigious paper

*by Nancy Salomon and Harvey Estes*

## ACROSS
1 Polish partner?
5 Figure for negotiation
10 Blue books?
14 Epitaph starter
15 1965 King arrest site
16 It's said with a raised hand
17 Color combo #1: Communist Beatles movie?
20 "Beats me!"
21 Town officials in New England
22 Not playing
24 Organic suffix
25 Bumps
28 The same
30 Volumes
35 Whiz
36 Wear a puss
37 Strauss opera
38 Color combo #2: Depressed Beantown nine?
41 Curtain call eliciters
42 Agnus ___ (religious figures)
43 Nice warm days?
44 Menachem's co-Nobelist
45 It may be stacked
46 Husky's burden
47 Millennium start
49 Long, long time
51 Art expert, at times
56 Stir up
60 Color combo #3: Cowardly IBM and GE shares?
62 Hamlet or Ophelia
63 Coty and Clair
64 401(k), e.g.
65 Took off on

66 "Golden Boy" dramatist
67 Gorge

## DOWN
1 Rough finish?
2 Big copper exporter
3 Qom home
4 It has its faults
5 Sugar suffix
6 Came clean
7 Smoke conveyor
8 Bull moose, to Roosevelt
9 Clear soup
10 Categorize
11 Hurt
12 ___ Reader (eclectic magazine)
13 That time
18 Word in a 16-Across

19 Colorless solvents
23 Side in a Colosseum battle
25 Obese "Star Wars" character
26 ___ squash
27 Further shorten
29 Musical exercise
31 Comedic Olsen
32 Metz's river
33 Act badly?
34 Popular high school class, informally
36 Have-not
37 Shoot up
39 F.D.R. project: Abbr.
40 Cover the floor anew
45 Gossiped
46 Nosy Parkers

48 Film intro?
50 Scrap
51 City on the Jumna
52 Play thing
53 Former Cosmos star
54 Harmonium part
55 "___ kleine Nachtmusik"
57 Bruins' home
58 32-card game
59 Crossword worker?
61 Old lottery org.

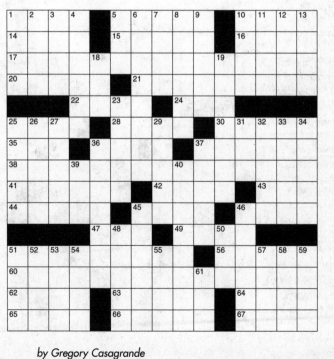

*by Gregory Casagrande*

# 18

## ACROSS

**1** 1692 witch trials setting
**6** Alan of "Manhattan Murder Mystery"
**10** Blues singer James
**14** Run off together
**15** Archaeological site
**16** Claim on property
**17** Dieting?
**20** Lady of Spain
**21** Haley who wrote "Roots"
**22** Function
**23** Distance runner
**25** Made big cuts
**27** Scottish cap
**30** Siamese ___
**31** Pal from Down Under
**32** Utah city
**34** Cry made while the reins are pulled
**36** Silly
**40** Going in a pit without a helmet?
**43** Mecca resident
**44** Allergic reaction
**45** Florence's river
**46** Many a Cecil B. DeMille film
**48** It may have an extra electron
**50** "Absolutely"
**51** Leftovers
**54** ___ Antoinette
**56** Live
**57** Misplace
**59** Does figure eights, e.g.
**63** Inn mergers?
**66** "What's gotten ___ you?"
**67** Wrapped up
**68** Minimal
**69** Superlative
**70** "Like taking candy from a baby!"
**71** Pompous ones

## DOWN

**1** Stitches
**2** Wings: Lat.
**3** Cut of meat
**4** English racetrack site
**5** Like grams and liters
**6** Coach Parseghian
**7** Moon-related
**8** Obsolescent phone part
**9** Actress Lansbury
**10** "A Nightmare on ___ Street"
**11** Traffic jam
**12** Drawn tight
**13** Chipped in
**18** Neighbor of Zambia
**19** Rare and wonderful
**24** Like some humor
**26** Five: Prefix
**27** Male turkeys
**28** Operatic song
**29** Waiter's card
**31** One of TV's Brady girls
**33** Mythical sorceress
**35** Frequently, to Frost
**37** Breezy
**38** Zero
**39** Slaughter of baseball
**41** Miniwave
**42** What Richard III offered "my kingdom" for
**47** Tristan's love
**49** Inventor Tesla
**51** Sir, in India
**52** Witch
**53** Catches one's breath
**54** Intends
**55** Overhangs
**58** Ancient portico
**60** Afternoon socials
**61** Scottish Gaelic
**62** Concordes
**64** Preschooler
**65** Shift, tab or caps lock

by James P. Sharp

## ACROSS

1 Understand
6 Ill-gotten gains
10 One of the Three Bears
14 With 59-Down, like some winds
15 Mimic
16 Shortstop Rodriguez
17 Invalidate
18 Beaujolais, e.g.
19 Swamp
20 Something followed on a screen
23 Sun or moon
26 64-Across and others: Abbr.
27 Blots out
28 Bet taker
30 Light snack
32 Astronomer Hubble
33 Jacques of "Mon Oncle"
34 Lazarus or Goldman
38 Something followed in a classic movie
41 Mediocre
42 Diner sign
43 Very angry
44 Violins and violas: Abbr.
45 Shoe part
46 French city on the Strait of Dover
50 Inc., in London
51 Boozer
52 Something followed at school
56 Medicine bottle
57 It goes across the board
58 Make into law
62 "¿Cómo ___?"
63 Dialing need
64 Whence the Ten Commandments
65 Dick Tracy's Trueheart
66 Try at roulette
67 It may follow a split

## DOWN

1 Govt. property overseer
2 Accepted the nomination, say
3 ___ Darrow of "King Kong"
4 Not much of a pencil
5 Trigger, e.g.
6 Hocks
7 Michael Jackson's record label
8 Filmmaker Riefenstahl
9 Not just fast-paced
10 Deadly African snake
11 Son of Sam, e.g.
12 Blackbird
13 Skating jumps
21 Colorado native
22 College sr.'s test
23 Follows
24 Roping venue
25 Some championship games
29 Narc's find, maybe
30 St. ___ (New York church, informally)
31 Inflammatory suffix
33 Aid to skiers
34 Goofs
35 Castle protectors
36 San ___, Calif.
37 Skilled
39 Divers' garb
40 Benevolence
44 "To ___ With Love"
45 Ice skater Midori
46 Spotted cat
47 Liqueur flavoring
48 Exams for would-be attys.
49 Book that readers think the world of
50 It's kept in a closet
53 Clip
54 Singer Tennille
55 Scissors sound
59 See 14-Across
60 Saturn or Mercury
61 Dead heat

by Sarah Keller

# 20

## ACROSS

1 Counterfeit
5 Innocent ones
10 Get steamed up
14 Landlocked ___ Sea
15 Hall of fame
16 Construction support
17 Wrongful act in Ankara?
19 Prosciutto purveyor
20 Letters of attorney?
21 Two-finger sign
22 Exclusive group
24 State of agitation
26 Surly sort
27 Longtime Susan Lucci role
29 Make pink?
33 Decoder feature
36 Loony
38 Looniness
39 Part of a plot
40 Garson of Hollywood
42 Cauterize
43 Wherewithal
45 Leaves home?
46 Sea swallow
47 J.F.K.'s 109
49 Sister of Clio
51 Johnstown disaster
53 Chihuahua wrap
57 Rarely seen haircut nowadays
60 Syndicate head
61 Neptune or Jupiter
62 Corporate image
63 Dud villages?
66 Old apple spray
67 Clear the slate
68 Le Pew of cartoons
69 On one's guard
70 Library device
71 Shade of blue

## DOWN

1 "___ Attraction"
2 Oranjestad's island
3 Gold standard
4 Kiwanian colleague
5 Dress option for cold weather
6 Start the pot
7 Telephonic 6
8 Canoe material
9 Begin a journey
10 Oily Cuban?
11 Over in Germany
12 Algeria neighbor
13 War of 1812 battle site
18 At any time
23 Well-kept
25 Conservative beauty?
26 Handled a reception
28 Brusque
30 Prayer joint?
31 Comeback to an accusation
32 Pull down
33 Drizzly
34 "Body Count" rapper
35 Burnoose wearer
37 Tea leaf reader
41 Logician
44 Skeptic's grain
48 Drove (around)
50 Keep an eye on
52 "Norma," for one
54 See eye to eye
55 "Where's ___?" (George Segal movie)
56 Collectible car
57 Blemish
58 Name spelled out in a 1970 hit
59 Seaweed substance
60 Teaspoon or tablet, say
64 Automobile accessory
65 Be decisive

by Richard Silvestri

## ACROSS

1 Whittler's material
5 Church benches
9 Knuckleheads
14 "Say it isn't so!"
15 Yoked beasts
16 Arcade game maker
17 Denver, the ___ High City
18 Humdinger
19 French Impressionist
20 Comment from a parent of rowdy sons
23 Diplomacy
24 Feel sick
25 Regard highly
28 Commercials
30 "Baseball Tonight" channel
34 Studies frantically
35 Insomniac's need
37 Bunion's place
38 Be unrealistically optimistic
41 Night bird
42 Earnings
43 Exposed
44 Binary digits
46 "Whew!"
47 Simple and unpretentious
48 $20 bill dispenser
50 Tennis's Steffi
51 Mellow person's motto
58 Reef material
59 Company V.I.P.'s
60 Brain wave
61 Grammarian's concern
62 The "A" in Chester A. Arthur
63 Sharp's counterpart
64 County of Newark, N.J.
65 Kind of sax
66 Snaky swimmers

## DOWN

1 Prebirth berth
2 Where the Reds and the Browns play
3 The "O" in ROM
4 Serves a sentence
5 Cry before "Open up!"
6 Rejoice
7 In good health
8 Give the cold shoulder
9 Disney deer
10 Peter of "My Favorite Year"
11 Kooky
12 Loads from lodes
13 Dog command
21 Poland's capital
22 Simplifies
25 Sound before "Gesundheit!"
26 Audibly overwhelm, with "out"
27 Syrup flavor
28 From another planet
29 Family rooms
31 Baby bird?
32 John, Paul and John Paul
33 Impoverished
35 Long story
36 Small, fast U.S. Navy craft
39 Beta's follower
40 Radioactive decay measure
45 Barbaric
47 California city
49 Old-fashioned news transmitter
50 Be a bad winner
51 What red ink indicates
52 Accts. for old age
53 Final Four org.
54 Brand of computer
55 Inactive
56 Calves' meat
57 Stops fasting
58 Pool stick

*by Peter Gordon*

## ACROSS

1 Light bulb unit
5 Up and about
10 Gung-ho
14 Like a 911 call: Abbr.
15 Captain Nemo's creator
16 Playing with a full deck
17 Group of packers?
19 High school breakout
20 Tiny bit
21 Afrikaner
22 Heavy smoker's voice, maybe
23 Use for expensive wood
25 Summer show, often
27 Certain sports event
30 Not on the up and up?
33 They may be picked up in bars
36 ___ McAn shoes
38 Casals's instrument
39 Friend of François
40 Group of freezer repairers?
42 The Buckeyes, briefly
43 You use gray ones
45 Think (over)
46 Have the lead
47 Borrowed
49 Michelangelo masterpiece
51 Toys on strings
53 Closing number
57 Down with something
59 Hostilities ender
62 Newsman Newman
63 Buddies
64 Group of masseurs?

66 Fluish feeling
67 N.B.A.'s Shaquille
68 Nonsmoking ___
69 After-bath wear
70 Humor columnist Dave
71 Lady's man

## DOWN

1 Modern news and entertainment source
2 Dean Martin's "That's ___"
3 George Bush, for one
4 Arm muscle
5 Student's stat.
6 Belgrade native
7 The Magi, e.g.
8 ___ circle
9 Wish undone
10 Usually
11 Group of airheads?
12 Rural retreats
13 Like a billionaire's pockets
18 ___-do-well
24 Some campus marchers: Abbr.
26 "Casablanca" cafe owner
28 Interrupter's word
29 Clean, as a spill
31 Designer Schiaparelli
32 Sullen
33 Crunchy munchie
34 End of grace
35 Group of male goats?
37 Timbuktu's land
40 "My word!"
41 Staff symbol

44 Visual survey
46 Bank fortifier
48 "Piece of cake!"
50 Seating section
52 Spa spot
54 With it
55 Some bedding
56 Conclude by
57 Practice punching
58 "Othello" villain
60 Smokey spotter
61 Way uphill
65 Noted cathedral town

*by Bob Peoples and Nancy Salomon*

## ACROSS

1 Scoring a 10 in gymnastics, say
5 A Muppet
9 Cloak-and-dagger person
14 Zoning minimum, maybe
15 Dear's partner
16 Remove, Soviet-style
17 Tees off
18 Site of some Sargents
19 ___ Gay (W.W. II plane)
20 Like a Muscovite at 5 p.m.?
23 Basketball "trophy"
24 Sch. on the Charles River
25 They're cast
27 Roundup terminus
31 Nouveau ___
33 Qatar bigwig: Var.
34 Short-billed rail
35 Barely beat
39 Helsinki mother's exhortation?
42 Suffix with towel
43 Penny-pinching
44 Makes better
45 Give the third degree
47 Torso
48 Shampoo bottle instruction
51 Whole lot
52 Suffix with percent
53 Game decider in Bangkok?
60 Attack
62 Pizazz
63 ★★★★ review
64 Mournful peal
65 Old-fashioned dance locale

66 Not windward
67 Looie's subordinate
68 Loose ___
69 Furnish for now

## DOWN

1 Worth a C
2 Neutral tone
3 Bellicose god
4 1979 Kinski title role
5 Involve
6 Wasn't erect
7 S.A.T. section
8 ___ O's (Post cereal)
9 Teleprompter's contents
10 20-, 39- or 53-Across, say
11 Home of the Black Bears

12 Leering sort
13 "Ode to Psyche" poet
21 ___ ware (Japanese porcelain)
22 Hong Kong neighbor: Var.
26 Swarmed
27 Eatery
28 Leave off
29 $50 Boardwalk outlay
30 Weasel out
31 Like some flushes
32 It's sometimes cast
34 Author Silverstein
36 Bo-o-o-o-ring
37 Chutzpah
38 Ultimatum word
40 Title "Mr." of a 1939 film
41 Lorelei's river

46 Maraca, essentially
47 Jerks
48 Puts on the line
49 "Maria ___"
50 Great name?
51 "Fun, Fun, Fun" car
54 Religious figure
55 1979–81 hostage site
56 Asia's ___ Sea
57 Do-re-mi
58 Not bumpy
59 Bassoon, e.g.
61 H.S. class

*by Sheldon Benardo*

## ACROSS

1 Steals from
5 Inferior, as writing
11 1936 candidate Landon
14 Norway's capital
15 Certain apartment
16 Hair styling stuff
17 Robert Mitchum drama, 1958
19 "___ Got You Under My Skin"
20 "Beetle Bailey" character
21 Big I.R.S. mo.
22 Out of the wind
23 Home of Bert and Ernie
27 Educ. group
30 Mal de ___
31 Feather's partner
32 Seniors' org.
34 Golf targets
37 Michelangelo masterpiece
41 Billy Wilder film starring Gloria Swanson
44 Fulton's power
45 ___ mater
46 Buffalo's lake
47 Kind of service
49 Charlottesville sch.
51 Chaney of horror films
52 A trusting person may be led down it
58 Millions of years
59 Calif. airport
60 Lhasa's land
64 In the past
65 Source of many old pop songs
68 Baseball score
69 Eight-armed creatures

70 Frolic
71 Rocker Tommy
72 Pop maker
73 Brake part

## DOWN

1 Goes bad
2 Dept. of Labor watchdog
3 Make less clear
4 The 40 in a "top 40"
5 Mao ___-tung
6 Karel Capek play
7 The "A" in James A. Garfield
8 Slippery ___
9 Citizen Kane's real-life model
10 Balance sheet abbr.
11 Spry
12 Embankment

13 Naval force
18 Consider
22 Get there
24 Small group of believers
25 Popular vacation isle
26 Cash register output
27 Quarterback's option
28 Drawn tight
29 "Rule Britannia" composer
33 Writings by David
35 D.C. type
36 Recapitulate
38 "Duke of ___" (1962 hit)
39 Wynken, Blynken and Nod, e.g.
40 Mideast's Gulf of ___

42 40-Down V.I.P.
43 Popular hand soap
48 Constabulary
50 Lead-in to girl
52 Oyster's prize
53 Scalawag
54 Hole ___ (golfer's dream)
55 "Ho ho ho" crier
56 Montreal team
57 "Rolling" things
61 Dull
62 Architect Saarinen
63 Toddler
65 Pull along
66 Gibbon, for one
67 Zippo

*by Holden Baker*

## ACROSS

1 Lash of oaters
6 Buccaneers' home
11 Iranian city: Var.
14 Bowl
15 "Are you calling me ___?"
16 Actress Merkel
17 Very best
19 "___ bin ein Berliner"
20 Gas of the past
21 Gore's "___ My Party"
22 Lullaby rocker
24 Amigo of Fidel
26 More acute
27 Scores for Shaq
31 Pianist Nero
32 Renée's pal
33 Police offer
35 Scattered
38 Wash cycle
40 Detergent brand
41 Close-fitting hat
42 Journey for Kirk
43 Where 17- and 61-Across and 11- and 29-Down might be used
45 Olympics chant
46 "Shush!"
48 Consumer's bottom line
50 Academic AWOL's
52 Gloppy stuff
53 Friars' fetes
54 Wilder's "___ Town"
56 Location
60 Swabber's org.
61 Ceaselessly
64 A.F.L.'s partner
65 ___ Kid of early TV
66 Like helium, chemically
67 Barbie's beau
68 Heads overseas?
69 Job extras

## DOWN

1 Lois of the Daily Planet
2 God of war
3 Sales force, for short
4 Use a key on
5 ___ Claire, Wis.
6 Ex-lax?
7 Word before fair or well
8 Cambridge univ.
9 More than thirsty
10 Noah's landfall
11 Fair exchange
12 Cry of surrender
13 Mr. Politically Incorrect
18 Pedro's lucky number?
23 Playground retort
25 "Take one!"
26 Wrist injury, maybe
27 Homer's boy
28 Mideast chief: Var.
29 Prerequisite
30 Gym garb
34 Tate collection
36 Hardly a he-man
37 Without ice
39 Gull-like predators
41 Josip Broz ___
43 Makes no attempt to save
44 Actress Pola
47 Not damaged
49 Trig function
50 Teamster's transport
51 "Sweet" O'Grady of song
54 Long ago
55 Roswell sightings
57 Roman's way
58 Istanbul native
59 CPR pros
62 Believer's suffix
63 Quick drink

by John F. Hughes

# 26

## ACROSS
1 Garlicky sauce
6 Mother __
10 Soft, white cheese
14 Like a depth finder
15 Financial page heading
16 Commentator Keyes
17 Pay, in a modern way
20 Adderley of bop
21 French painter Charles Le __
22 Wee
23 Fire
24 Show interrupter
25 Make a disclosure
29 Mrs., in Barcelona
32 Letter before beth
33 Trauma ctrs.
34 "It's So Nice to Have __ Around the House"
35 Sweater letter
36 Word with mass or mixed
38 Arabian plateau region
39 Work without __
40 Fleischer in Washington
41 Sign for an audience
42 Part of Roy G. Biv
43 Cause pain or numbness, maybe
46 Traffic marker
47 "Family Ties" role
48 Colt .45's, now
51 Film rating org.
52 Proof's end
55 Upstage everyone, maybe
58 __ bath

59 Big model
60 Unoriginal
61 Long basket, in hoops lingo
62 Put the end first?
63 Evaluated, with "up"

## DOWN
1 Org.
2 "The Music Man" setting
3 "Step __!"
4 Collagen injection site
5 Cool dip?
6 Nader's 2000 running mate
7 Dark clouds, say
8 One coming out
9 Emigrant's document
10 Met squarely
11 Verve
12 Pine products
13 "Handy" one
18 Enemy leader?
19 Shade of blue
23 Mar. honoree
24 Actress Polo of "Meet the Parents"
25 Agent Swifty
26 "Prince Valiant" princess
27 Threw a party for
28 Of Hindu scriptures
29 Makeup problem
30 A Gandhi
31 Wrestling's __ the Giant
34 New wing
36 Trunk
37 Fish-eating flier
41 Theatrical shorts

43 Betting group
44 Come to pass
45 Jai __
46 Cuckoo
48 __ prof.
49 The big house
50 French bean?
51 Boss's writing
52 Interrogate
53 Art Deco artist
54 Scout's doing
56 Med. plan
57 TNT part

by Steve Jones

## ACROSS

1 Maker of Space Invaders
6 Cut with scissors
10 Verdant
14 Batman's sidekick
15 "Voilà!"
16 Gazetteer datum
17 Punch in the mouth
20 Locale
21 Clean air org.
22 Lovers' secret meetings
23 "___ está usted?"
25 Roller coaster cry
26 Token punishment
32 Not tacit
33 Billy Joel's "Tell ___ About It"
34 Sgt., e.g.
35 Pooped out
36 Boeing 747, e.g.
37 The Jetsons' dog
39 Royal flush card
40 Cheerios grain
41 Bordeaux wine
42 Having drinks
46 They're exchanged at the altar
47 "So what ___ is new?"
48 Sitting room
51 Iceland's ocean: Abbr.
52 It's $24 on Marvin Gardens
56 Item for an armed detective, maybe
59 Chimney grime
60 Lake touching four states
61 French city, in song
62 Moppet
63 Caboose's spot
64 Dag Hammarskjöld, for one

## DOWN

1 Clumsy boats
2 Singer Braxton
3 Border on
4 Low-calorie snack
5 Calligrapher's purchase
6 Walk over
7 Shuttle org.
8 Neighbor of Wyo.
9 Black cat
10 Perry Mason or Ally McBeal
11 "QB VII" author
12 Splinter group
13 Triumphant cries
18 Iced tea garnish
19 Didn't stand pat
24 Newspaper's ___ page
25 Sharpen
26 It might be put on the rack
27 "Two Women" star Sophia
28 Letter before iota
29 Preface
30 It has a groovy head
31 Choo-choo's sound
32 Pierce
36 Fancy sports cars, for short
37 "___ fair in love . . ."
38 Portable cutter
40 Not in stock yet
41 String quartet instrument
43 Weaken with water
44 Screen favorite
45 Infernal
48 "Hey, you!"
49 Sailor's greeting
50 Piece next to a knight
51 Opera highlight
53 French 101 verb
54 Require
55 Orchard unit
57 Poetic preposition
58 Turntable turners, briefly

by Peter Gordon

# 28

## ACROSS

1 Plays the ponies
5 Dads
10 Suitcase
14 Part of Hawaii
15 Make amends
16 Philosopher Descartes
17 Unleashes
19 Penny ___
20 What the neophyte jester didn't feel like?
22 Building addition
24 Bagel topper
25 Officeholders
26 Curtain holder
27 Fashion
30 Relative of a rabbit
32 Common term for strabismus
35 Bill
36 What the part-time abacus user didn't feel like?
40 Likely
41 And so forth
43 Relative of a rabbit
45 God of war
46 Tire filler
47 Hold up
48 German cathedral city
50 Castaway's place
52 What the queasy rodeo rider didn't feel like?
57 Savior, to Bach
58 "Family Affair" star of 1960's–70's TV
61 "Jeopardy!" host Trebek
62 Reached in a hurry
63 Rock band Better Than ___
64 Gardener's need
65 Thrown for ___
66 Pond duck

## DOWN

1 Big Apple subway inits.
2 ___ de cologne
3 Puccini's last opera
4 Because
5 Magician's hiding spot
6 At the peak of
7 Gene group
8 Founder of Scholasticism
9 Take care of
10 Tennis's Steffi
11 "Le Moulin de la Galette" artist
12 Chant
13 Strips
18 White ___
21 Sigh with relief, say
22 Bow
23 Writer Ephron
27 Accomplishment
28 Popeye's Olive ___
29 Direct (to)
31 Touch
33 Get really wet
34 A twin city
35 Twitches
37 Dined
38 Not shrunk or enlarged
39 Tribe with palisaded villages
42 "Jeopardy!" host Fleming
43 Big citrus fruit
44 Sacred birds, to some
45 Unprincipled
47 Indian prince
49 The Balance
50 Opposite of "Yum!"
51 ___ shooting
53 Elegance
54 Boy, in Barcelona
55 Flying mammals
56 Spanish articles
59 ___-la-la
60 Shakespearean prince

*by Steven Dorfman*

## ACROSS

1 They may be jerked
6 Leisurely time to arrive at work
11 Sounds at a masseur's
14 Ten sawbucks
15 Deposed leader, perhaps
16 Web search result
17 Cereal for squirrels?
19 Ethyl ender
20 Distribute anew
21 Vicente Fox's country: Abbr.
22 Miami-___ County
23 See 34-Down
25 Evaluated
27 Like the lunar surface
31 Enrapture
32 Down for the count
33 Become established
35 Jocks' antitheses
38 Tuck away
40 Hunk of fairway
42 Shade of red
43 Sunni's belief
45 Expressed orally
47 The Mustangs' sch.
48 Wasn't straight
50 Prepares for a rough ride
52 Olympics vehicle
55 Clinton's birthplace
56 Oodles
57 "A jealous mistress": Emerson
59 Tens, perhaps
63 Natural leader, in astrology
64 Perfumed actress?

66 One who can't pass the bar?
67 Penalized
68 Advance in age
69 Silver-gray
70 Most mall rats
71 Site of two famous banks

## DOWN

1 Lasting impression
2 "___ bitten . . ."
3 "I ___ it!": Red Skelton
4 Motionless
5 Legislative houses
6 Business card abbr.
7 Physical, e.g.
8 Some sneaks
9 Joan's "Dynasty" role
10 ___ amis
11 Futuristic woman's chapeau?
12 Yoga practitioner
13 Hardly cheap
18 Erupted suddenly
22 Star in Cygnus
24 Fix, as a pool cue
26 Buddhist sect
27 "___ fan tutte"
28 Where wheels roll
29 Island's source of revenue?
30 Temperamental types
34 With 23-Across, a guiding light
36 Prefix with god
37 Leave speechless
39 Place for a spare tire?
41 Doughnut-shaped

44 Sportscaster Allen
46 Mini-pooches
49 Snookums
51 Kind of league
52 Corkwood
53 Dinner substitutes
54 Hive member
58 Some feds
60 Opposed to
61 Boxer Spinks
62 New Year's word
64 Time in 65-Down
65 Want ___

by Fred Piscop

# 30

## ACROSS
1 Pilfer
6 Mars' counterpart
10 Waiflike
14 French wine valley
15 Expert
16 Texas city on the Brazos
17 Bearer of the heavens, in myth
18 Memo abbr.
19 Bullfight cheers
20 Craziness
23 Pigs' digs
24 French friend
25 Lowly abode
28 Stomach muscles, for short
29 Talk like th-th-this
33 Most-wanted invitees
35 "___ bin ein Berliner"
36 Rubik of Rubik's cube fame
37 No-goodnik
41 ___ a one
42 Observe
43 Any Time
44 Happy-go-lucky syllables
46 ___ Francisco
48 Men
49 Money for old age: Abbr.
50 South-of-the-border friend
52 Slight hoarseness
59 "I do" or "Drat!"
60 One way to settle a dispute
61 It's just over a foot
62 Sandpaper coating
63 And others: Abbr.

64 Alfred E. Neuman, for one
65 Back talk
66 Former mayor Giuliani
67 Sports figures

## DOWN
1 Extra fat
2 Tiny bit
3 Cheerful tune
4 Vulgar
5 Say "um . . ."
6 Some marbles
7 Baseball's Babe and others
8 Old Harper's Bazaar designer
9 Lie on the beach, perhaps
10 Common soda bottle capacity
11 Football game division
12 Cake decorator
13 Prying
21 Penpoint
22 Earthbound bird
25 Lacks, briefly
26 Of an armbone
27 Princess' headwear
29 Coll. or univ.
30 Reduce to ruins
31 Result
32 Tournament of ___
34 Features of some bright rooms
35 Suffix with Israel
38 New York hockey player
39 Teachers' org.
40 Cotton fabrics
45 Jackie's second

46 Odoriferous
47 Spot in a river
50 Leading
51 "Ready ___ . . ."
52 Reasons for lighthouses
53 ___ avis
54 Singer Redding
55 Ballerina's dress
56 Gumbo ingredient
57 Tons
58 Column next to the ones

*by Patrick Merrell*

## ACROSS

1 Purple bloomer
6 Hardly tanned
10 Vegan's no-no
14 Staffordshire stench
15 Factual
16 First name in scat
17 Dire early morning warning?
20 Sort
21 Ga. neighbor
22 Takes potshots
23 Used up
25 Cools down
26 Doll's cry
28 Big cheeses
32 Author Jong
34 Do damage to
35 To and __
38 Joey's place?
42 "Lah-di-__!"
43 Kauai keepsakes
44 Pan-fry
45 Most fearless
48 Golfer's selection
49 Hood's blade
51 Snitches (on)
53 Orbital high point
55 Blood fluids
56 Jefferson Davis's org.
59 Buzz over New York City animals?
62 Powerful shark
63 Enlarge, as a hole
64 Spooky
65 Gaelic tongue
66 __ a soul
67 Lively dances

## DOWN

1 Centers of activity
2 Teen fave
3 Yale person?
4 Diving bird
5 Rugged box
6 "Right away!"
7 Long, long time
8 Little shaver
9 New wings
10 Army docs
11 Skip the big wedding
12 Balm additives
13 Highland hats
18 Fender blemish
19 Riddles
24 Nafta, for one
26 Pinochle combo
27 Diva's delivery
29 Part of a lunar cycle
30 Newsman Rather
31 Nonprofit's U.R.L. ending
33 Here, there and everywhere
35 Gettysburg Address opener
36 Old newspaper section
37 Foreboding
39 Fish caught in a pot
40 Tease
41 Alternative to air or highway
45 Often-stubbed digit
46 Hot and humid
47 Status before statehood: Abbr.
49 Asparagus unit
50 Sounds of frustration
52 Los Angeles hoopster
53 Pinnacle
54 Make, as money
55 Debate (with)
57 Make dirty
58 Home of Iowa State
60 Pasture
61 Tappan __ Bridge

by Barry Callahan

## 32

### ACROSS
1 Stick on a spit
7 "M" director Fritz
11 Sun. speech
14 Shop worker
15 Takeoff artist
16 ___ polloi
17 Lawgivers
18 900-line psychic Miss ___
19 It may be worn under a tunicle
20 "It's getting late!" abroad?
23 Kofi ___ Annan
25 CD-___
26 Kind of star
27 Token of welcome
28 It may be taken with a raised hand
30 Nothing, at a poker table
32 Upper-left key
33 "Tristia" poet
35 Long distance letters
36 "What'll you have?" abroad?
41 Morsel for Dobbin
42 Taunt
43 It's twice-eaten
45 Rushed violently
49 Old saying
50 Old NOW cause
51 Early computer
52 O'Hare monitor abbr.
54 Go to and fro
55 "Baloney!" abroad?
59 Crackpot
60 Horse of different colors
61 Ringmaster's place
64 ___ de France

65 Two tablets, say
66 "Psst!" follower, perhaps
67 Days of yore
68 Agenda, informally
69 Excessive

### DOWN
1 T.G.I.F. part
2 Lea call
3 Many a conventiongoer
4 Hilo hello
5 Yakutsk's river
6 Once, once
7 Milk: Prefix
8 Poise
9 Not e'en once
10 Airline gang
11 Cascades peak
12 Windblown
13 Like Playboy cartoons
21 Stu of early TV
22 Mumbai master
23 Schooner filler
24 New Ager John
28 Coloratura's asset
29 Humpty Dumpty-shaped
31 Pseudopod former
34 Understand, slangily
37 Odin, to the Germans
38 Hemp source
39 Diner freebie
40 Pervasive quality
44 Dennis or Doris
45 Tush
46 Exciting

47 Smashed windows, maybe
48 Adulterate
53 Got into shape
54 Aid in aiming
56 Captured
57 Term paper abbr.
58 Tarzan's transport
62 Montana motto starter
63 Zip

*by Kumar Balani*

## ACROSS
1 Garage sale tag
5 The whole spectrum
9 Sea creatures with claws
14 Worker's ___ (insurance)
15 Catch rodeo-style
16 "Scheherazade" locale
17 Knight's protection
19 Quite sharp
20 Marisa of "What Women Want"
21 Bad firecracker
22 James Dean persona
23 Econ. yardstick
25 Letter distribution on base
27 "Close, but no cigar"
31 Mermaid's home
32 Phone the folks
34 Despot
38 ___ Khan
39 Sheetful of cookies
41 Twinings product
42 Italian cheese
45 Money for the house
48 Fellows
49 Certain spiders in "Spider-Man"
50 Linguistic borrowing
55 Moo ___ pork
56 Fouled up
57 "___ you sure?"
59 Ice house
63 Treat badly
64 Theme of this puzzle
66 "Hasta la ___, baby!"
67 NBC's peacock, e.g.

68 Sitting on one's hands
69 Gas additive
70 Smudge
71 Loch ___

## DOWN
1 It's got your number: Abbr.
2 London shopping district
3 Muslim holy man
4 Big name in catalogs
5 Pitcher's pride
6 Warty hopper
7 Poppy product
8 Mrs. F. Scott Fitzgerald
9 Pride of country music
10 Indy entry
11 Island near Curaçao
12 Tropical nut
13 Whiff
18 Final inning, usually
24 Gratis, to a lawyer
26 Land bridge
27 Raleigh's state: Abbr.
28 Othello's undoer
29 Chowder morsel
30 Vocalist Sumac
33 Biblical verb ending
35 Plenty, and then some
36 In apple-pie order
37 Shades from the sun
40 See 65-Down
43 General pardon

44 F.D.R.'s plan
46 Code of conduct
47 Rowan & Martin's show
50 Sailor's shore time
51 Planet's path
52 In ___ (hurriedly)
53 R.&B. singer Lou
54 Start to wilt
58 It follows that
60 Put on board, as cargo
61 Lubricates
62 Small bills
65 With 40-Down, a modern company

*by Nancy Salomon and Harvey Estes*

# 34

## ACROSS

1 High school outbreak?
5 Afternoon affairs
9 Witty Wilde
14 Person of action
15 Sitar master Shankar
16 Fern-to-be
17 Rapscallions
18 McCain's state: Abbr.
19 Spills the beans
20 Thomas Mann classic
23 Home of the Braves: Abbr.
24 Photo ___ (camera sessions)
25 See 48-Across
28 Bakes, as eggs
30 Place for pennies
32 Inc., abroad
33 Angry
35 Classic toothpaste
37 Halving
40 Partner of dined
41 Golfer's concern
42 Jiffy
43 "Gotcha!"
44 "ER" extras
48 With 25-Across, speaker of the quote hidden in 20-, 37- and 53-Across
51 Watch chain
52 Abba's "Mamma ___"
53 Nearby
57 Dunkable treat
59 Hamlet, e.g.
60 Old English letters
61 Grenoble's river
62 Astronaut Shepard
63 Newshawk's query
64 Passover supper
65 Tuna ___
66 Newbie

## DOWN

1 Nike competitor
2 O'Neill title ender
3 Himalayan denizen
4 Start with while
5 Walked about
6 Brings in
7 Tel ___
8 XXL, e.g.
9 Old port on the Tiber
10 #, to a proofreader
11 Deli dish
12 Object of Indiana Jones's quest
13 In medias ___
21 Abominable
22 A.T.M. maker
26 ___ time (never)
27 Nutritional fig.
29 Tear apart
30 Coup d'état group
31 Seaweed, for one
34 Drop a line?
35 Spirits that victimize the sleeping
36 Wing: Prefix
37 Prie-___ (prayer bench)
38 Not level
39 Like a lamb
40 Financial daily, initially
43 Bat wood
45 Shop with an anvil
46 Choice word
47 Refuses
49 Habituate
50 Out-and-out
51 Big test
54 Dutch cheese
55 Greece's ___ of Tempe
56 Adult eft
57 Speak ill of, in slang
58 Sugar suffix

*by Paula Gamache*

## ACROSS

1 Treaty subject
5 Broadway's Bob
10 Org. of which Nancy Lopez was once champion
14 Hang over one's head
15 For the birds?
16 Neighbor of Azerbaijan
17 Prediction basis #1
19 Author ___ Neale Hurston
20 Biblical landfall
21 Diving bird
23 Chess champ before and after Botvinnik
24 Hem again
25 Prediction basis #2
28 60's campus org.
29 Card balance
31 Draws out
32 Old yellers?
34 Was second-best
35 Prediction basis #3
38 English painter John
40 Buttinskies
41 Prod
44 Robt. E. Lee, e.g.
45 Côte ___, France
48 Prediction basis #4
50 "The Three Faces ___"
52 Car ad abbr.
53 Hoop grp.
54 Wept wildly, maybe
55 Ties up the line

57 Prediction basis #5
60 Suffix with stink
61 Cause to swell
62 Adriatic resort
63 Like a pinup
64 Check mates?
65 Toil wearily

## DOWN

1 Sacred places
2 Laughed loudly
3 Swampy area
4 Chocolaty campfire treat
5 Almanac bit
6 Egg cells
7 Lady's man
8 1978 Peace co-Nobelist
9 Guarantee
10 Gossipy Smith

11 The right stuff?
12 Some sale sites
13 Assayer, e.g.
18 Cheaply showy
22 Sent to the mat
25 Cases the joint for, say
26 Way out
27 Slow times
30 Frozen Wasser
32 Angler's basket
33 Tart fruits
35 Container with a lid that flips
36 Voyage beginning?
37 Self-confidence
38 Power problems
39 Whip up
42 Vintner's prefix
43 Moguls

45 Micromanager's concern
46 Carry too far
47 Football blitz
49 Safe place
51 Nincompoops
54 Takes in
56 Sauce source
58 Promise to pay
59 The "one" of a one-two

*by Sherry O. Blackard*

# 36

## ACROSS

1 Listened to
6 Nickname for a good ol' boy
11 Entrepreneur's deg.
14 "The Goat" playwright Edward
15 Zones
16 Seek office
17 Etiquette expert
19 Wager
20 They're not yet adults
21 Conductors' sticks
23 Head of a fleet
26 Colorful crested bird
27 Photocopier attachment
28 Rice dish
29 Part of a printing press
30 Least good
31 Actress Peeples
34 Solicits for payment
35 Organ features
36 10-percenters: Abbr.
37 W.W. II region: Abbr.
38 Eiffel Tower's home
39 Falling sound
40 Rabbit's home
42 Mississippi city where Elvis was born
43 Alcohol
45 Reveals secrets about
46 "I'm in a rush!"
47 Lessen
48 Suffix with schnozz-
49 Language mangler
54 ___ and vinegar
55 Boner
56 Weeper of myth
57 Office seeker, for short
58 Raises, as children
59 Not on the perimeter

## DOWN

1 Popular Easter dish
2 Inventor Whitney
3 Stomach muscles, briefly
4 Breathers
5 More reserved
6 Trite
7 Coffee vessels
8 "Busy" one
9 Free of pointed parts
10 Military offensive
11 Famous tap dancer
12 ___ Vista Lake, Calif.
13 Anxious
18 On ___ with (equal to)
22 ___ Aviv
23 Parenthetical comment
24 Food with a hole in the middle
25 One with encyclopedic knowledge
26 Exposes
28 Stop by
30 Electrical lines
32 From Rome: Prefix
33 ___ Martin (auto)
35 Back section of seats
36 Dessert often served à la mode
38 More fastidious
39 Islamic chiefs
41 Bush spokesman Fleischer
42 Dabbling duck
43 Busybody
44 Old disease
45 Skiers' transports
47 Love god
50 Mex. lady
51 Rubbish
52 ___-Wan Kenobi
53 Paper Mate product

*by Norman Wizer*

## ACROSS

1 Not that
5 Plods along
10 Take it easy
14 Open to inspection
16 Showy flower
17 Citrus fruit waste
18 Coal deposits?
19 Thieves' hangout
20 Employee's reward
21 Hippie's catchword
22 Intrinsically
23 Place for a cold one
24 Play time
27 A.L. division
31 A criminal may go by it
32 Stomach filler
34 Log-burning time
35 D.E.A. operative
36 Theme of this puzzle
37 Ship lockup
38 Allergy consequence
39 Field of expertise
40 The "L" in 51-Down
41 Erne or tern
43 Radio talk show participant
44 L.B.J.'s successor
45 Tree knot
47 Throw out
50 April forecast
51 Santa ___, Calif.
54 Lena of "Havana"
55 Q-Tip, e.g.
57 Come down
58 Ruin a shot, in a way
59 Water swirl

60 Mexican bread
61 "Ah, me!"

## DOWN

1 Walked (on)
2 Call to Fido
3 "Terrible" czar
4 Lust, for one
5 Takes an oath
6 ___ lazuli
7 More than heavy
8 Jubilation
9 French seasoning
10 Philadelphia tourist attraction
11 Pavarotti specialty
12 Brass component
13 North Carolina motto starter
15 Exit
21 Give a scathing review

22 Sweet drink
23 Hospital capacity
24 Indian royalty
25 Make jubilant
26 Around
27 Drink with fast food
28 Like Mayberry
29 Well's partner
30 Cubist Fernand
32 Explorer maker
33 Be beholden to
36 Country dance spot
40 Adam's apple's place
42 Dennis the Menace, e.g.
43 Rapids transit?
45 Microsoft honcho
46 Explosion maker
47 Shoe bottom

48 Decked out
49 Cheese coating
50 Wander
51 Mil. truant
52 Canaveral letters
53 Beame and Saperstein
55 ___ a plea
56 Baden-Baden or Évian

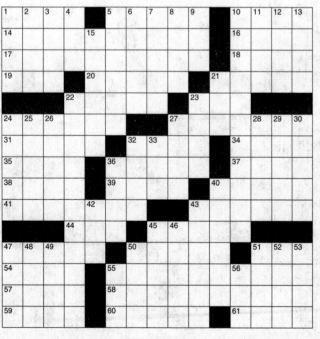

*by Ed Early*

# 38

## ACROSS

1 "Belling the Cat" author
6 Kind of code
11 New Year overseas
14 Ignorance, they say
15 Love of Livorno
16 Word of farewell
17 Start of a quote by John Kenneth Galbraith
19 Reunion group
20 Cousin of a foil
21 Unearthly
22 Sander part
23 Not the first transaction
25 Register
27 Quote, part 2
32 Tried to stop from scoring
36 Surgically bind
37 Jewish month
38 Actor Stephen
40 Times to call, in ads
41 Society stalwart
44 Goal-oriented sorts
47 Quote, part 3
49 Item for a fairy?
50 Brings to a boil?
55 Switch's partner
57 Early computer language
60 Math computation
61 Resistance unit
62 End of the quote
64 Draw upon
65 Choir's platform
66 Africa's largest country
67 Rocky hill
68 Take care of
69 Gregg expert

## DOWN

1 A Yokum
2 Split to unite
3 Many end in .com
4 Actor Milo
5 Trident-shaped letter
6 Summon
7 Mideast bigwig
8 More meddlesome
9 Magazine store?
10 Charlemagne's crowner
11 Depart
12 Satan's doings
13 Carnival sight
18 Has to have
22 Lahr co-star of 1939
24 PC linkup
26 Stat for Sosa
28 Mal de ___
29 "Gibraltar may be strong, but ___ are impregnable": Emerson
30 Cato's way
31 Capone's nemesis
32 Johnny of "Ed Wood"
33 Director Petri
34 40-hour-a-weeker
35 Mama Cass ___
39 King of Judah
42 From ___ Z
43 Valens who sang "Donna"
45 Sacred song
46 Writer Fleming
48 Pick out
51 Full range
52 Chip away
53 Showed over
54 Refuse
55 Event on a card
56 Facetious "I see"
58 A Maverick
59 Other, in Acapulco
62 Ones of the highest grade: Abbr.
63 Highway curve

by Alan Olschwang

## ACROSS
1 Eye amorously
5 No ifs, ___ or buts
9 Partners
14 Place for seagulls to sit
15 Not shallow
16 Oven emanation
17 "What ___ is new?"
18 Dance in a grass skirt
19 Neglected neighborhoods
20 Classic Salinger novel, with "The"
23 Poi root
24 Yang's complement
25 Favorite project
28 Make, as a guess
31 Land for a house
34 Without help
36 Tijuana gold
37 Celebration
38 Behave promiscuously
42 Erupt
43 Bemoan
44 Put back to zero, say
45 Electric fish
46 Goulash seasoning
49 Make an effort
50 1040 initials
51 Old-fashioned containers
53 Repeated lyric in a children's song
61 Clay brick
62 "Incredible" one
63 Follow orders
64 Neighbor of Earth
65 Comedic actress McClurg
66 Took a train, say
67 Beauty, brawn or brains
68 "I haven't a thing to ___!"
69 Egg holder

## DOWN
1 Letters from the Persian Gulf?
2 Southwestern river
3 For fear that
4 Put up
5 Cling (to)
6 Brain cell
7 Supermarket part
8 C-___
9 #5 iron
10 "Over the Rainbow" composer Harold
11 Studio visit
12 TV honor
13 Enclosure with a MS.
21 Any port in a storm
22 Mountainous area of Austria
25 No longer in fashion
26 Secretly tie the knot
27 Dry (off)
29 ___ of London
30 Mentalist Geller
31 Opposite of most
32 Playful animal
33 Cantankerous
35 This instant
37 Goliath, to David, e.g.
39 Use the backspace key
40 Break bread
41 Toped
46 Mass figure
47 Firenze's land
48 Field goal specialist
50 Fill (with)
52 Heap ___ upon
53 Coffee, slangily
54 Middle of March
55 Starts of workweeks: Abbr.
56 Not just swallow whole
57 Ill-mannered
58 Clarinet's kin
59 Cincinnati nine
60 Russian rejection

*by Gregory E. Paul*

# 40

## ACROSS

**1** Underwater predator
**5** Letters on a Soyuz rocket
**9** October stones
**14** Fermented honey drink
**15** Bona fide
**16** Running wild
**17** Indigo dye source
**18** School for a future ens.
**19** NBC staple since 1/14/52
**20** Either 38- or 53-Across
**23** Privy to
**24** Pizarro's prize
**25** Clod buster
**28** Priests' subordinates
**31** Automobile sticker fig.
**34** Boredom
**36** Trucker's truck
**37** Fly high
**38** "The Last Supper" artist
**42** Battering wind
**43** Out ___ limb
**44** Largish combo
**45** In the style of
**46** Tableland
**49** Hosp. units
**50** Iron man Ripken
**51** Ten: Prefix
**53** "The Divine Comedy" author
**60** Canon competitor
**61** Grease monkey's job
**62** The "S" in CBS: Abbr.
**63** Muse of poetry
**64** Bruins' sch.
**65** First name in jeans
**66** Surrenders
**67** Deportment
**68** "Baseball Tonight" channel

## DOWN

**1** Barbra's "Funny Girl" co-star
**2** Philosopher Descartes
**3** Genesis son
**4** He finished second to Ike
**5** Friend of Friday
**6** Big name in small planes
**7** Scene of Jesus' first miracle
**8** Blueprint
**9** Many John Wayne films
**10** TV teaser
**11** Verdi heroine
**12** It can generate a lot of interest
**13** Porker's pad
**21** Land of a billion
**22** Line dance
**25** Hägar's wife, in the comics
**26** N.B.A.'s Shaquille
**27** ___ Gay (plane)
**29** Zagreb resident
**30** Suffix with fact
**31** Three-card hustle
**32** Indiana hoopster
**33** Dixie dish
**35** Arles article
**37** [not a typo]
**39** Esther of "Good Times"
**40** Heredity helix
**41** ___ for (substantiate)
**46** Feeling of pity
**47** Unlike toadstools
**48** Cyclades' sea
**50** Big bill
**52** Airplane seat option
**53** Calamitous
**54** Part of 18-Across: Abbr.
**55** Reunion attendee
**56** ___ Baines Johnson
**57** Ogles
**58** Invitation letters
**59** "Put ___ writing"
**60** Boom box button

*by Matthew J. Koceich*

## ACROSS

1 Kindergarten lesson
5 1957 Literature Nobelist
10 Lay an egg
14 Source of caffeine
15 Valuable violin
16 First-sight phenomenon
17 Top 10 hit for the Impressions, 1964
18 Leaves for lunch?
19 Out of port
20 Russia's cold war beer?
23 She played Ginger on "Gilligan's Island"
24 Corona's end
25 Weather changer
28 Site of El Misti volcano
30 Self starter?
33 Nifty
34 Destiny
35 Diminutive suffix
36 Deep-sea brew?
40 Cable network
41 Leave the sack
42 Unit charge
43 ___ roll (sushi selection)
44 Basketball Hall-of-Famer Archibald
45 Plower's creation
47 Shade of black
48 Wide-eyed
49 Presidential pint?
55 Go cold turkey
56 Laughing
57 Overcast
59 Suffix with kitchen
60 Opening words
61 Shade of green
62 Action figure?
63 None of the above
64 Where county offices are

## DOWN

1 Blotter letters
2 Long pass
3 Laine of jazz
4 Holiness
5 James Bond locale
6 Whirlpool competitor
7 Many a beer
8 Its motto is "Industry"
9 Pistols and swords
10 Instant
11 Red ink amount
12 Through
13 Shade of green
21 They're all in the family
22 Customary
25 Provide
26 Flat agreement
27 Fleet-related
28 Bel ___ cheese
29 Gaelic tongue
30 "King Olaf" composer
31 Look after
32 Sprinkle around
34 Make stockings, say
37 One of the Jacksons
38 Haydn's "The Seasons," e.g.
39 Calls before a court
45 Divisor
46 "Yech!"
47 2000 World Series M.V.P.
48 Art style
49 Mercury or Saturn
50 Lo-cal
51 Salon request
52 Biblical verb
53 War of 1812 battle site
54 F.D.R.'s Scottie
55 Mathematician's sign-off
58 To this day

by Richard Silvestri

# 42

## ACROSS
1 Male voice
5 Destroy
9 Ralph ___ Emerson
14 Gem with a play of colors
15 Scores to shoot for
16 Love affair
17 Lawman of the Old West
19 Hindu queen
20 Home on the range
21 Old West cemetery
23 Off-road transport: Abbr.
25 Family girl, for short
26 Burn
30 Construction piece
33 Winter clock setting in S.F.
36 Grand lineup
37 Location of 21-Across
39 Weaver's apparatus
40 Durable fabric
41 Upon
42 Location of 51-Across
44 Explorer Sir Francis
45 Music with jazzlike riffs
46 Electric dart shooter
47 Twisty turns
48 ___ tai
49 Boo-hoo
51 Site of a famous gunfight
56 Squiggly marks
61 Not suitable
62 Legendary lawman of the Old West
64 Mow down
65 Art Deco artist
66 Poet Pound

67 Neighbor of a Finn
68 Nostradamus, reputedly
69 Take five

## DOWN
1 Boxing match
2 Church alcove
3 Ditto
4 Smack
5 Discombobulate
6 "Count me out"
7 Lackluster
8 Capital once known as Christiania
9 1941–45, for the United States
10 Nanking nannies
11 Actress Anderson
12 Event done at 20 paces, maybe

13 Pitcher Hershiser
18 Word before "set, go!"
22 Missouri river
24 MTV features
26 Seasons, as steak
27 Petty thief
28 Wonderful smell
29 Suckling sheep
31 Shouldered
32 Trimming tools
33 Sandwich breads
34 Stir up, as a fire
35 Uses a Smith Corona
38 Mustang and Impala
40 Connector of floors
43 Scare suddenly
44 Amount to subtract

48 Bike that zips
50 Glossy brown fur
51 Fixes a squeak
52 Had a gut feeling
53 Bat's hangout
54 Amazes
55 Instrument for a Muse
57 Wanton look
58 Muddleheadedness
59 Flubs
60 Tiff
63 Gobbled up

*by Sherry O. Blackard*

**43**

## ACROSS
1 Lady's shoe
5 Diamond measure
10 Prefix with legal
14 Phone button below the 7
15 Egg-shaped
16 Lighted sign
17 Delhi wrap
18 Information-gathering mission
19 Gin flavoring
20 Wall Street Journal beat
23 Many a legal holiday: Abbr.
24 Bill-blocking vote
25 Sapporo sash
28 Spoon-___
30 Part of a play
31 Call to Bo-peep
34 Macintosh and others
38 Deep sleep
39 Luau dish
40 Fly traps
41 Those not on the guest list
46 King: Lat.
47 Fire remnant
48 Stud site
49 Things that go together
50 To's reverse
51 Chest protector?
53 What 20-, 34- and 41-Across have in common
61 Photographed
62 Newsman Newman
63 One for the road
64 Keokuk's home
65 Chaucer pilgrim
66 Diver Louganis
67 Legally invalid

68 Not so crazy
69 What fellers need

## DOWN
1 "Hey, you!"
2 D-Day beachhead
3 Filly's mother
4 Spectrum creator
5 Princess topper
6 ___ plaisir
7 Billiard hall item
8 Proton's place
9 Period of occupancy
10 Annoying, as a gnat
11 Wheel connector
12 Side-splitter
13 Polished off
21 Soy product
22 "Darn it!"

25 Come about
26 Wilderness Road blazer
27 Blend
29 Pool measure
30 In reserve
31 Sounds from R2-D2
32 Stroll along
33 Good thing
35 Zero-star review
36 Fish eggs
37 It's "company"
42 Diversify
43 Certain similar chemical compounds
44 Burns, to Allen
45 ___ the Red
50 Of the unborn
52 Acts the blowhard

53 Biblical pronoun
54 Vigorous protest
55 Creative spark
56 Verdon of "Damn Yankees"
57 Honeycombed home
58 Atmosphere
59 Ragout or burgoo
60 Takes most of
61 Pride or lust

*by Nancy Kavanaugh*

# 44

## ACROSS

1 Cuts blades
5 Slack-jawed
10 Fit together
14 Sound return
15 Cut up
16 Photographer's setting
17 Photograph bands?
19 1963 role for Liz
20 In concert
21 Dallas sch.
22 Out in front
23 Writer
24 Make a video about lowlifes?
26 More just
29 Sparkler
30 Old inits. in telecommunications
31 Tire filler
35 Sorry to say
39 Censor's target
41 Problem-solving advice appropriate for this puzzle?
42 "Liquor is quicker" poet
43 Pueblo Indian
44 Pilot, slangily
46 Cultural funding org.
47 Close one
49 N.Y.S.E. alternative
51 Take pictures of heads?
57 IV units
58 OPEC land
59 Catwoman, to Batman
60 Meteorological effects
63 Where to get off
64 Make an X-rated movie, perhaps?
66 Dumb cluck
67 Jazzman Shapiro
68 Score after deuce
69 Old-fashioned knife
70 Certain cup maker
71 Epitomes of busyness

## DOWN

1 Arizona city
2 Publisher Adolph
3 Celebrate noisily
4 Cornhusker archrival
5 Shade of blonde
6 Hamlet's father, e.g.
7 Bouquet
8 Give some zing
9 Newspaper staffers, for short
10 Guy's guy
11 Noted blind mathematician
12 It may be let off
13 Gangsters
18 Basic belief
22 Leave 5-Across
25 Spurs
26 School group?
27 Prefix with sphere
28 Mess up
32 La Paz's land: Abbr.
33 Ultra-aloof
34 Gist
36 One-sided victory
37 Cruising
38 ___ attack
40 What a child may stand on
45 Millionaire's transport
48 Attorney's org.
50 Egyptian beetle
51 Mushers' vehicles
52 Resigned president
53 Put up with
54 In flames
55 Nick of "Affliction"
56 Some playoffs
61 Aunt Bee's boy
62 ID's for the I.R.S.
64 Where achievers go
65 "What'd I tell you?!"

by Nancy Salomon and Bill Zais

## ACROSS

1 Instrument with a bow
6 Trucker with a handle
10 Like stallions and bulls
14 Heavenly hunter
15 Sharpen
16 Touched down
17 Two for breakfast?
20 Play ___ (do some tennis)
21 Deuce, in tennis
22 Baltimore player
23 Mink or sable
24 Not as dusty
25 Taiwan's capital
29 Stout drinks
30 Money in the bank, say
31 A ___ apple
32 Mailed
36 Two for dinner?
39 Ponies up
40 Summer coolers
41 Redhead's dye
42 "You said it!"
43 Diviner, of a sort
44 All-night studier
48 "Psst!"
49 What cable TV renders unnecessary
50 Bambi's mother, for one
51 Without cost
55 Two for dessert?
58 Isle of exile
59 Pro or con, in a debate
60 Dumbwaiter, essentially
61 Radiator sound
62 "Don't move!"
63 Actress Moorehead

## DOWN

1 ___-Cola
2 Libido, in psychiatry
3 Vitality
4 Place for hay
5 Loved ___
6 Head of a meeting
7 Radius or rib
8 Finale
9 Aromatic
10 Craze
11 "March comes in like ___ . . ."
12 Fine thread
13 It'll knock you out
18 Needle case
19 War god
23 Crumbly white cheese
24 Ad biz awards
25 Push (down)
26 Away from port
27 Brit's exclamation
28 Beloved animals
29 Colorado town on the Roaring Fork River
31 Venomous snake
32 Fret
33 Almost forever
34 State bird of Hawaii
35 Peter I, II or III
37 How some shall remain
38 Chips ___! (cookies)
42 Asian nurse
43 Owner's proof
44 Sleeveless wraps
45 Spools
46 Riyadh residents
47 Flaky minerals
48 Sweetie pie
50 Bit of baby talk
51 Symbol of the WB network
52 Bit attachment
53 Relieve
54 Ambulance grp.
56 "Take a load off!"
57 When repeated, a Latin dance

*by Janice M. Putney*

# 46

## ACROSS

1 Shoe blemish
6 Sean Connery, for one
10 Plod along
14 Trivial objection
15 Grandma
16 Like some tales or orders
17 Mountain ridge
18 Uzis and AK-47's
19 Columnist Bombeck
20 Barely wound Lee's men?
22 Affirm
23 Math course, briefly
24 Intertwine
26 ___ room (place for tots)
30 Van Gogh home
32 Skater's jump
33 Ricky player
35 Skylit lobbies
39 Elude capture
41 Primal therapy sounds
43 Beachhead of 1/22/44
44 Dance at a barn dance
46 Braun and Gabor
47 "Julius" in Gaius Julius Caesar
49 Join the navy, say
51 Major publicity
54 Weight not charged for
56 Airline to Ben-Gurion
57 Examine an Eastern European language?
63 Moreno of "West Side Story"
64 To laugh, to Lafayette
65 One-tenth payment
66 Oast
67 More than
68 Per ___ (yearly)
69 Bohr or Borge
70 Many a Bosnian
71 Lots and lots

## DOWN

1 Heroin, slangily
2 Mystery writer John Dickson ___
3 Iris's place
4 Irish surname starter
5 Lamb's cover
6 Traffic problem
7 Venezuela's capital
8 "Gentle ___ Mind" (country classic)
9 Mortarboard attachment
10 Pilfer I-beams?
11 Caterpillar, e.g.
12 Ancient Mexican
13 Menacing look
21 Italy's largest lake
25 In the area
26 Sitar selection
27 Yoked pair
28 City on the Moselle
29 No-frills Cessna?
31 Greet the day
34 Brontë heroine
36 26-Down player Shankar
37 "___ corny . . ."
38 Kind of prof.
40 Moth's temptation
42 Office worker
45 One on the way in
48 Computer shortcuts
50 Sweet stuff
51 Judean king
52 Three-time batting champ Tony
53 Like Cheerios
55 Sour-tasting
58 Busy place
59 Fan's publication, for short
60 Sicilian spouter
61 Ground-up bait
62 Clothes lines

by Eugene W. Sard

## ACROSS

1 North African capital
6 Fit one inside another
10 Bit of change
14 Farsi speaker
15 Linchpin site
16 Bibliography abbr.
17 Religious artwork
18 Sidesplitter
19 Actress ___ Flynn Boyle
20 More out of control?
23 Boot reinforcement
25 When it's broken, that's good
26 Cyclotron bit
27 Cousin of a caribou
28 Database operations
31 Goosy
33 Long in the tooth
35 Bill's partner
36 M.B.A. holder, maybe
37 Not as tall?
43 Shindigs
44 It may be brewing
45 Not aweather
46 Blouse ruffle
49 Conductor Sir Georg
51 Jet ___
52 Latin 101 word
53 Notable period
55 Punches in
57 More secure?
61 Mirth
62 Baal, e.g.
63 Cut into
66 Turkish money
67 1986 #1 hit by Starship
68 Outpost group
69 Magi's origin
70 North Carolina college
71 Nasal dividers

## DOWN

1 Letters sometimes inscribed above a name
2 Press secretary Fleischer
3 Traveler's guidebook
4 Prank
5 Royal toppers
6 D.E.A. agent
7 Way out
8 Some fore-and-afters
9 Prefix with hydrozoline
10 Bologna home
11 Bologna home
12 Actor Brando
13 Comedienne Boosler
21 Noteworthy periods
22 Bring up-to-date
23 Kind of spirit
24 "Three Sisters" sister
29 Milne youngster
30 Old TV sidekick
32 Nick's wife
34 Pedestal part
36 Lunar locale
38 Tribal symbol
39 Sinuous swimmer
40 Basketball maneuver
41 Close
42 They're tapped
46 Sound of keys
47 Bloomer who popularized bloomers
48 Shaded recesses
49 Flip-flop, e.g.
50 Coastal features
54 Union demand
56 ___ Haute, Ind.
58 Place in the House
59 Former P.M. of 11-Down
60 Pearl Buck heroine
64 URL part
65 Raters of m.p.g.

by Janet R. Bender

# 48

## ACROSS

1 West Point institution, for short
5 Made a gaffe
10 Bathroom powder
14 Enter
15 Exit
16 Is in arrears
17 Quick race
20 Sisters' daughters
21 It's connected to the left ventricle
22 Sportscaster Garagiola
24 Sault ___ Marie
25 Basketball hoop
27 Patriotic women's org.
28 Insurance company with a duck in its TV ads
30 Lament
32 Engine additive letters
33 Munchie in a brownie, perhaps
35 Doesn't wander
37 Rock band with the platinum album "The Downward Spiral"
41 Sleeping disorder
42 Kind of valve in a car
44 "Leaving ___ Vegas"
47 Commit to memory
49 Spacey of "American Beauty"
50 Granola morsel
51 Egyptian reptile
52 Praiseful poem
54 Big galoot
55 Eventual oak
57 Imaginary
59 1979 nuclear accident site
64 Pay attention to
65 Gift recipient
66 Onetime Atlanta arena
67 At loose ___
68 Oodles
69 Light blade

## DOWN

1 "How revolting!"
2 Old French coin
3 Liza . . . with a Z
4 "Me, myself ___"
5 Put into power
6 Cash in
7 Suntanners catch them
8 Sister of Zsa Zsa
9 Architect Mies van ___ Rohe
10 Kind of list
11 Medals and trophies, e.g.
12 Vampire in Anne Rice novels
13 D flat's equivalent
18 Salvation for someone stranded in the Arctic, say
19 "Whatever Lola Wants" musical
22 Long feature of a crocodile
23 In the blink ___ eye
25 Book after Judges
26 Citizen of Tehran
29 Ballerina Pavlova
31 Recognition from "the Academy"
34 Food spearers
36 Location
38 ___ tide
39 Groovy light source
40 Gambol
43 Chemical suffix
44 Despise
45 German city near the Belgian border
46 In an attic
48 "Really, you don't have to"
53 Towels off
56 Dark wines
57 Bone by the humerus
58 Balm ingredient
60 Physicians, for short
61 Quadrennial games org.
62 SSW's reverse
63 Casino cube

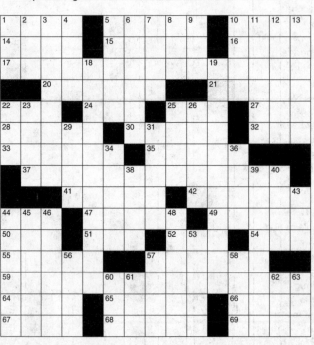

by Trip Payne

## ACROSS

1 Lines on a musical staff
6 Froth
10 Man trapper
14 Maui veranda
15 First name in scat
16 Needle holder
17 Muscle
18 Tibetan monk
19 Launch agcy.
20 Columnist for the lovelorn
23 Part of U.C.L.A.
24 Square-dancing call
25 Maximally
29 Strike callers
31 Shot onto a green
32 Columnist for the lovelorn
38 Citadel student
40 Texas tea
41 Pago Pago's place
42 20-Across, to 32-Across
45 Rumor generator?
46 "Trick" joint, maybe
47 Brunch dish
49 Beverage that soothes a sore throat
53 "Be Prepared" org.
54 Entreaty to 20- or 32-Across
61 Popeye's tooter
62 High time?
63 Autumn drink
64 Ode or haiku
65 Shirt brand
66 Go __ with
67 Addition column

68 Addition column
69 Trappers' wares

## DOWN

1 Napoleon was banished to it
2 Dress
3 __ B'rith
4 Deputy __ (cartoon canine)
5 Important exams
6 Chops down
7 Norwegian saint
8 __ mater
9 The Kettles
10 Morning Star
11 Video game pioneer
12 Pondered
13 Softly, on scores
21 Teeny bit

22 Petty officers
25 Depositor's holding: Abbr.
26 Spring occurrence
27 Longish skirt
28 Dentist's direction
29 Bring together
30 Fr. miss
33 Beak
34 Title for Agatha Christie
35 Actor Jannings
36 Something to play
37 Put (away)
39 Expressed disapproval
43 Irritated
44 Parks on a bus
48 Like the Marx Brothers
49 Hulking herbivore

50 Burger topper
51 Portable dwelling
52 Abounds
53 Gives a bit
55 Seep
56 It may be new or blue
57 Awful-tasting
58 Britney Spears, to teen girls
59 Euro part
60 Work units

*by Kelly Clark*

## ACROSS

1 Father's offering
5 What will be
9 Not try very hard
14 Gator's kin
15 Tennis score after deuce
16 Completely anesthetized
17 Fashionable explosive?
19 Team track event
20 Tuba sound
21 Airline to Israel
23 From __ Z
24 Fashionable view?
28 Took in with astonishment
29 Chanel of fashion
30 Clinches
31 Insolence
33 Marriage guide
37 Neighbor of Aus.
38 Fashionable dessert?
41 Justice Fortas
42 Sun Valley state
44 Splashy resort
45 Plodded
46 Friendly femme
49 New York tribe
51 Fashionable substitute?
55 Gardner on screen
56 Shaving stuff
57 "O Sole __"
58 Relatively red
60 Fashionable conveyance?
65 Like some remarks
66 Vincent Lopez's theme song
67 Garr of "Tootsie"
68 Undue speed
69 Make one's permanent mark?
70 Lyrical tributes

## DOWN

1 Roast hosts, briefly
2 Recliner part
3 Ongoing saga
4 Set-tos
5 Terrif
6 Brouhaha
7 Kitchen counter?
8 As a whole
9 Fancy twist
10 United
11 Statesman Stevenson
12 Defense grp. of 1954–77
13 Check for fit
18 Impact sound
22 Mil. mail drop
24 Walked nervously
25 Film composer Schifrin
26 Quarreling
27 Discouraging words
28 Leslie Caron role
32 Gateway sales
34 Tough
35 W.W. II torpedo craft
36 Cold war foe
38 Out of jeopardy
39 Grp. of books in the Bible
40 Welles's "Citizen"
43 Kramden laugh syllable
45 Connect with
47 Wall St. debut
48 Pal of Jerry Seinfeld
50 Madame Bovary
51 Strident
52 The Donald's first ex
53 Rue de Rivoli city
54 Comeback to "Are too!"
59 Buffalo's summer hrs.
61 R.N.'s forte
62 "Go team!"
63 High dudgeon
64 Carol contraction

*by Nancy Salomon*

## ACROSS

1 North Pole assistant?
4 Military bases
9 Lowly workers
14 Misstatement
15 In the upper berth
16 Brightest star in a constellation
17 Holiday ___
18 Postal device
19 Scent
20 Star of 36-Across
23 Insurance company worker
24 What an actor waits for
25 Terrier or retriever
28 Deli sandwich
29 Trails
32 Titled lady
33 Use an 18-Across
35 Kind of position
36 Series set at 328 Chauncey Street in Brooklyn
41 Wise one
42 Computer shortcut
43 All over
44 Put up, as a building
46 Sharp flavor
50 Sun. speaker
51 Wrath
52 "I agree!"
53 Co-star of 36-Across
58 About 39 inches, in England
60 Multiflavor ice cream
61 Touch of frost
62 Letter opposite 16-Across
63 Conspicuous success

64 WNW's opposite
65 Mass transit vehicles
66 Spicy sauce
67 Wilmington's state: Abbr.

## DOWN

1 Hebrew prophet
2 Amount of space in a newspaper
3 Foil user
4 Suggest
5 First word in a fairy tale
6 Male deer
7 Turnpike charge
8 Oration
9 Not in anymore
10 Tickle Me ___
11 When no games are scheduled

12 Flyers' and Rangers' org.
13 Mule of old song
21 Ability
22 Vienna's home: Abbr.
26 Sharif of "Doctor Zhivago"
27 Hair goops
29 Wrestling win
30 Six, say, for a first-grader
31 Herb in soups
32 Signified
34 Long, long time
35 In favor of
36 Leader opposed by the Bolsheviks
37 Sharpen
38 Boosts
39 Bub

40 World Series mo.
44 "To ___ is human . . ."
45 ___ Pieces
47 Made good
48 In any way, in dialect
49 God's honest truth
51 Think tank output
52 Mediterranean land
54 Goad
55 Blue Triangle org.
56 Steelmaking site
57 Gay 90's and Roaring 20's
58 Mafia
59 Big bird

by Allan E. Parrish

# 52

## ACROSS
1 Lay to rest
6 Up to, informally
9 Zest
14 Riyadh resident
15 Prefix with cycle
16 According to
17 Black Panthers, e.g.
19 Like Valhalla's heroes
20 "A-Tisket, A-Tasket" singer
22 "___ a deal!"
23 Victor's booty
24 "We want ___!" (baseball fans' cry)
26 ___ Speedwagon
27 Piece of field artillery
31 Was ill with
34 Faint with beating heart
36 Place for a béret
37 Like the Tower of Pisa
39 Hardship
40 Stuck in Pamplona?
41 Pro ___
42 Old Ford flop
44 Draft dodgers' bane: Abbr.
45 This puzzle's theme
48 Fallen space station
50 Concerning, in memos
51 Nail-___ (tense situations)
54 Catch some rays
56 Rite of passage, for some
59 ___ Fountain
61 Pertaining to tautness
63 Black ink item
64 Bard's before

65 Barely managing, with "out"
66 They're sometimes stolen
67 Match part
68 Actress Zellweger

## DOWN
1 Doctrine
2 Artless ones
3 Dutch bloomer
4 Perry White, e.g.
5 Most elegant
6 Counterparts to lyrics
7 Verb type: Abbr.
8 Actress Kudrow
9 Father of independent India
10 Hope's road show org.
11 Wine drinks
12 Dry run
13 Miners' finds
18 Luminous
21 Some post-graduate study
25 "Tell ___ the judge!"
27 Young toughs
28 Teller's stack
29 Vacation times in Verdun
30 Some M & M's
31 Mata ___
32 Rat-___
33 Blonde's quality, in jokes
35 Ran a tab
38 Croquet area
40 More showy
43 Broadcasts
46 Asteroids' paths
47 New Deal org.
49 Annul
51 Stanford-___ (I.Q. rater)
52 Arrested
53 Classic Ladd western
54 Attempt
55 Celestial bear
57 Numbered hwys.
58 Insignificant
60 Neckline shape
62 T-shirt size: Abbr.

*by John R. Conrad*

## ACROSS

1 Currency substitute
6 Big party
10 The Beatles' "___ Madonna"
14 Japanese verse
15 Part of A.M.
16 Yellow spread
17 When many people have cookouts
20 Formerly
21 They average 100
22 Free
23 Bug
24 Enter
25 Spanish snack
28 Monopoly game token
30 Novelist Rona
35 Flamenco cries
36 It's nothing, really
37 Big name in beauty products
38 Frédéric Auguste Bartholdi creation
41 People in People
42 Energy
43 Uno y dos
44 Pittsburgh's Mellon ___
45 Speaker in the Baseball Hall of Fame
46 Henry of the House Judiciary Committee
47 Emperor who poisoned Britannicus
49 Singer Sumac
51 Feeling pins and needles
55 Santa ___
56 Unagi, at a sushi bar
59 Tablet inscription on 38-Across that commemorates 17-Across

62 Up to snuff
63 Actress Skye
64 Home on the range
65 Take a breather
66 Mmes., in Madrid
67 Embellish

## DOWN

1 Painful place to be kicked
2 Sugar source
3 Fairgrounds attraction
4 War-hero president
5 Iris's center
6 Makes verboten
7 What's more
8 Walk over
9 Artist Toulouse-Lautrec
10 "Stay" singer Lisa
11 Designer Gucci
12 Person with a list
13 Go up and down rapidly
18 Zebras, e.g.
19 Grifter's ploy
23 Buckle
24 One who works on a swing
25 Puccini opera
26 Adjust
27 "The Power of Positive Thinking" writer
29 Carnival city
31 1986 self-titled soul album
32 Boat to Staten Island
33 In the cards
34 "Family Ties" mom
37 Not really sing
39 Congo border river

40 Aloha shirt accessory
45 Aftershock
48 Graceland name
50 Island south of Sicily
51 Open slightly
52 Part of an IV
53 Troubles
54 Da's opposite
55 Pair in a dead man's hand
56 Montreal player
57 Penultimate fairy tale word
58 Bank holding
60 Modern courtroom evidence
61 Marked, as a ballot

by Peter Gordon

# 54

## ACROSS

1 Fraud
5 Yemeni or Qatari
9 Coffee lightener
14 Show bravery
15 Over hill and ___
16 Oscar-winning Berry
17 Coal waste
18 Stir up
19 French clerics
20 Symbol marking a composer's music?
23 Early form of bridge
24 Waikiki wreath
25 Leave
28 Crossword solving, for one
32 Make happy
33 Land of O'Kelly and O'Keeffe
35 Woman's hairstyle
36 Composer's popular works?
40 Choose
41 Emulated Pinocchio
42 Close, in poetry
43 Gets hot under the collar
46 Spirited
47 Publicize
48 Powell of the Bush White House
50 Like the dog days of summer, for a composer?
56 Brilliance
57 One of five Norwegian kings
58 Thoroughly
60 Portion
61 Cry of greed
62 Writing of Chaucer
63 Marine detector
64 Ages
65 Verve

## DOWN

1 60's protest grp.
2 Baby elephant
3 Asia's ___ Sea
4 It can provide a big jolt
5 Skillful
6 What the monsoon season brings
7 Parcel out
8 "It's ___ real!"
9 Pursues
10 Cottontail
11 Exile isle for Napoleon
12 One of the Baldwins
13 Fit well together
21 Flung
22 African antelope
25 Show cars
26 Leave via ladder, maybe
27 Stickum
28 ___ Piper
29 "Peer Gynt" dramatist
30 Background sound in a store
31 Door
33 Oklahoma city
34 1 or 95: Abbr.
37 Heads-up
38 10-Down fur
39 Deluge
44 Noted Las Vegas casino
45 Disorderly one
46 Toils (away)
48 Hue
49 John who wrote "Butterfield 8"
50 Hardy heroine
51 Cuatro + cuatro
52 Pearl Buck heroine
53 Volume
54 And others, for short
55 "Damn Yankees" seductress
59 Kind of Buddhism

by Sheldon Benardo

## ACROSS

1 "Whatcha ___?"
5 Madonna musical
10 "Yikes!"
14 Big name in oil
15 Assaults with a spray
16 "Adam ___" (Eliot novel)
17 Elvis Presley hit of 1956
20 Hippie
21 Without support
22 Like Coolidge's utterances
23 Letter adornment
25 Volcanic spew
27 Gist
29 Portly plus
32 Record player
34 Losing tic-tac-toe row
35 Pre-stereo
36 Stared at
37 Busy airport
38 Gluck's "___ ed Euridice"
39 Hanging on every word
40 Standard
41 Ralph Kramden, for one
42 Sturdy tree
43 Bluesman McClinton
45 Mos. and mos.
46 Workout venues
48 Purple ___, New Hampshire's state flower
50 Very, to Verdi
52 Reject, as a motion
55 Beatles hit of 1967
58 "The Little Mermaid" baddies
59 Pitchfork wielder
60 Diversion
61 Box that crackers go into?
62 Hair-raising
63 British P.M. before Macmillan

## DOWN

1 Children's author Roald
2 Nabisco cookie
3 Four Tops hit of 1965
4 Scandinavian land, to natives
5 Mission
6 Fluctuates
7 Cake finisher
8 Kind of party
9 One way to get directions
10 Carlo Levi's "Christ Stopped at ___"
11 Rolling Stones hit of 1965
12 Yemeni port
13 Expunge, as text
18 Sewer line?
19 Fast runner
23 Stuck-up sort
24 Prefix with system
25 Really love
26 "Love Story" author
28 Outlying community
30 Words after bend or lend
31 Cel mates?
33 Widebody, e.g.
35 ___ Smith's pies
37 Haarlem painter Frans
38 Start-up costs
40 Shooter pellet
41 Easily provoked
43 A fifth of MMMX
44 Medicine show purchase
47 Parson's estate
49 Actress Woodard
50 Impresses
51 Long Island Railroad stop
52 Opera persona
53 England's Great ___ River
54 Plump songbird
56 E.R. workers
57 "Hold on a ___"

by Robert Malinow

# 56

## ACROSS

1 Monopoly square
5 Palladium, for one
10 Dumbfound
14 Biblical preposition
15 Not only like
16 Oscar Wilde poem "The Garden of __"
17 Hubbub
18 About
19 Heist haul
20 Twelve inches of supply boat?
22 Break, in a way
23 "The Great Ziegfeld" co-star
24 Raspy
26 Quiver holder
30 Target of some collars
32 Out of this world?
33 Three feet of basketball floor?
38 Refrain syllables
39 Tasteless
40 Apple spray
41 Three miles of climbing vine?
43 Stopper
44 Pizzas
45 Bamboozled
46 Stoolies do it
50 Thai's neighbor
51 Bee or Em
52 39.37 inches of stream?
59 A dirty person may draw one
60 Foaming at the mouth
61 It's long in fashion
62 "__ From Muskogee"
63 Place for an urn
64 Flower of one's eye?
65 Show partner
66 Library device
67 "Valley of the Dolls" actress

## DOWN

1 Like some deserts
2 Stud stake
3 Take __ stride
4 Lady's man
5 Long-vowel mark
6 Enlighten
7 El Cordobés adversary
8 Sacramento's __ Arena
9 Coriaceous
10 River feature
11 Sounding like lions
12 Skyrockets
13 First name in cosmetics
21 Pizazz
25 Bit in a horse's mouth
26 Lesser Sunda island
27 Patron saint of Norway
28 Guileful
29 Square __
30 Try hard to visualize
31 New Testament book
33 It may be rattled
34 Fish story
35 Lyricist Lerner
36 Haymaking aid
37 Historic Scott
39 It speeds up flights
42 Org. that may be involved in a cleanup
43 Bust alternative
45 Calling
46 Cousin of a clog
47 Temblor
48 Up to
49 Waters of Hollywood
50 Oblivion
53 Horne solo
54 Boor's lack
55 Radiate
56 Butler's quarters?
57 Way out
58 Piece of high ground

*by Richard Silvestri*

## ACROSS

1 Slice (off)
4 Indoor camera attachment
9 Rand McNally book
14 Gay 90's, e.g.
15 Spooky
16 One of the Allman Brothers
17 Prefix with puncture
18 Alfalfa's love in "The Little Rascals"
19 A-list group
20 "Freeze!"
22 Leader of reformers' 31-Down
24 Wet, weatherwise
26 Charged particle
27 Processes, as ore
29 Daily Hollywood publication
33 Signals goodbye
34 Sent a letter by phone
35 Playboy Mansion guy
37 The best three in a three-of-a-kind
38 Goofed
39 Concrete
40 One over a birdie
41 Use
42 Succinct
43 Using a blowtorch
45 Give
46 Fill one's stomach
47 Oscar winner Marisa
48 Leader of football's 31-Down
53 Dutch cheese
56 Stadium
57 Farsi speaker
59 Dolly the clone, e.g.
60 Nobleman
61 Snooped (around)
62 Operated
63 Skew
64 Wagner work
65 Pink Floyd co-founder Barrett

## DOWN

1 Mrs. Rabin of Israel
2 Killer whale
3 Leader of pop music's 31-Down
4 G-man, e.g.
5 Gets smart
6 Ordered set
7 Pie-cooling spot
8 Mound
9 Throat tissue
10 The Green Wave, in college sports
11 With 54-Down, in reserve
12 Poker stake
13 Crystal ball user
21 Grimm works
23 Employed
25 "___ in his kiss" (1964 pop lyric)
27 Exchange
28 Parrot's cousin
29 Airline to Rio
30 Skater's jump
31 1960's group (in three different ways)
32 Brewer's need
34 Drescher of "The Nanny"
36 Turn tail
38 Musical with the song "Buenos Aires"
39 Girl's name meaning "born again"
41 Not budging
42 Mr. Turkey
44 "Instant Karma" singer
45 One of Santa's reindeer
47 Needle
48 Needles
49 Like some medicines
50 Zeus' wife
51 The Flintstones' pet
52 Plummet
54 See 11-Down
55 Darn
58 It borders Wash.

by John Leavy

## ACROSS

1 Argentine plains
7 "Some of this, some of that" dish
11 School advisory grp.
14 Everlasting, old-style
15 The "C" in U.P.C.
16 Serving of corn
17 1925 musical featuring "Tea for Two"
19 Opposite of post-
20 Blue books?
21 Stereo forerunner
22 Number 2's
24 Make jubilant
26 Fish organ
27 Of one's surroundings
30 Hard to miss
33 1950's–60's guitar twanger Eddy
34 Get __ (start work)
36 Ed of "Daniel Boone"
37 Like Shostakovich's Symphony No. 2
38 "I've Got the Music in Me" singer, 1974
41 Eggs
42 March Madness grp.
44 Stet's opposite
45 Quiz show host, often
47 Make a point, in a way
49 White knights
51 Les États-__
52 UFO occupant
53 Barber chair attachment
55 Sashes in "The Mikado"
56 Opera set along the Nile

60 Reaction to a back rub, maybe
61 Polynesian treat
64 Brooklyn campus, for short
65 Furies
66 Off course
67 Shade tree
68 Cloud __
69 Insufficient

## DOWN

1 They used to be lowered into wells
2 Nuclear energy source
3 Restaurant handout
4 Amino acid chain
5 Lee who founded the Shakers
6 Mariner
7 Part of an act
8 Oz visitor
9 Summer D.C. setting
10 Crop-destroying beetle
11 1937 Jean Gabin title role
12 Infield cover
13 Mars' counterpart
18 Like a road in a Frost poem
23 Charles Lamb's pen name
25 Soup ingredient
26 Golden __
27 Tennis scores after deuce
28 Chew (on)
29 Liquor-flavored cake
30 Go askew
31 Emphatic refusal
32 Winter Palace residents

35 ". . . __ the cows come home"
39 Bad time for Caesar
40 House overhang
43 The New Yorker cartoonist Peter
46 Original "Ocean's Eleven" star
48 1972 Ben Vereen musical
50 Bridal paths
52 Invective
53 Store sign
54 Follow
55 Store sign
57 "I'd consider __ honor"
58 Collision memento
59 Like would-be bohemians
62 Mentalist Geller
63 Semicircle

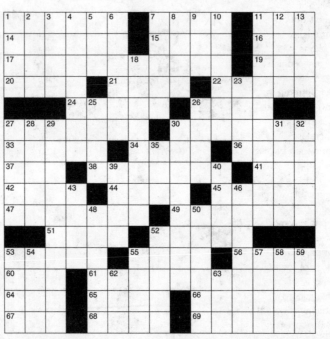

*by Ed Early*

## ACROSS

1 Construction co. projects
6 Chicago-to-Memphis dir.
9 Fighting
14 Lecherous looks
15 X
16 River past Liechtenstein
17 Father of the Pleiades
18 Some California baseball stars?
20 Ostracize
21 Propelled a lifeboat
22 Classic pop
23 California baseball players in trouble with the I.R.S.?
25 Hollywood, with "the"
26 Ace place?
27 Locker room item
29 Cause of a stomachache
33 Some noblemen
34 Gang of California baseball players?
37 Garlic piece
39 Company made famous by Pong
40 Brings on board, in a way
41 Like some inspections
46 Pack animal
47 What brainy California baseball players get?
51 Takes advantage of
53 Front wheel alignment
54 O.K. Corral figure
55 California baseball teammates?
57 Mother of Pebbles
58 PC letters
59 Start of Julius III's papacy
60 First name in 2000 news
61 Lets
62 What a contact contacts
63 Bangladesh's capital, old-style

## DOWN

1 Good times
2 "___ Weapon"
3 Like the presidential suite
4 Starbucks size
5 Draft org.
6 Lean person
7 ___ Khan (tiger in "The Jungle Book")
8 Dentist's request
9 The Diamondbacks, on scoreboards
10 Comparison word
11 Sipping sites
12 Where soldiers may be busy
13 Adjusts, as a cap
19 Mdse.
21 Newbery Medal winner Scott
24 Small eggs
27 Involved with
28 "Silent" prez
30 Civil War letters
31 "Mangia!"
32 Messenger ___
34 Equestrian
35 Adam's apple picker
36 Common injury location
37 Writer buried at Westminster Abbey
38 Supple
42 Down Under girl
43 It leans
44 Runway
45 Madrileño's land
47 Regular: Abbr.
48 The Velvet Fog
49 Like marshes
50 Plane seating request
52 Fast-moving card game
56 Hirt and Hirschfeld
57 Get a wife

by Peter Gordon

## ACROSS

1 Comical Laurel
5 All excited
9 Knights' ladies
14 Sexologist Shere
15 Sandy slope
16 "Remember the ___!"
17 Service status
18 Damon of "The Bourne Identity"
19 Disinfectant brand
20 Wind pointer
23 D.D.E.'s command in W.W. II
24 Some household heads
25 Not Rep. or Dem.
26 Myrna of "The Thin Man"
27 The hoop in hoops
28 Having good posture
30 Hissy fit
32 Meal in a shell
33 Quoits target
35 One ___ kind
36 Lay ___ the line
37 "Changing the subject . . ."
41 Raid rival
42 Pi follower
43 China's Sun ___-sen
44 Take a load off
45 Part of CNN
47 Flies alone
51 Leave dumbstruck
52 Confederate soldier
53 Lobbying grp.
55 Before, of yore
56 Ford or Lincoln
57 1972 Carly Simon hit
60 City near Syracuse
62 Stink to high heaven
63 Brain wave

64 Russian Revolution leader
65 Patiently wait
66 Dryer outlet
67 Rival of ancient Sparta
68 Winter blanket
69 Pay to play

## DOWN

1 Missourian's demand
2 Musical ineptitude
3 "Relax, soldier!"
4 Shipshape
5 Product pitchers
6 Some football linemen
7 Airing
8 "Stop worrying about picayune stuff!"

9 Big name in Chicago politics
10 Prince ___ Khan
11 Grand Prix racer
12 :-) or :-(
13 Wise king of Israel
21 Woo in an unwelcome way
22 ___ public
29 Rooters' refrain
31 At all, in dialect
32 Connect with
34 Island on the Java Sea
37 Free serving at a restaurant
38 A bull may wear one
39 Many a commuter's base
40 Explorer ___ da Gama

41 Storied vampire
46 Popular swimwear
48 Hard to lift
49 Show the ropes to
50 100-member group
52 "___ Hope" (former soap)
54 Cockeyed
58 Horse halter?
59 Cheer starter
61 A.F.L.'s partner

*by Harvey Estes and Nancy Salomon*

## ACROSS

1 Couch
5 Fail to act
10 Host before Carson
14 Grad
15 Think the world of
16 Light brown
17 Sask. neighbor
18 ___ palm
19 Whiz kids
20 Hoot at confined hooters?
23 Bank statement amt.
24 Have a bite
25 Eventually
27 Explorer Johnson
30 Captain's hook
33 Send via Western Union
34 Hamlet, in "Hamlet"
36 Bill Gates, to some
38 Supplies, as assistance
41 Claim Confederate leader has varied taste?
44 Winetaster's criterion
45 1970 Kinks hit
46 Triumphant cry
47 Room at San Quentin
49 Part of a basilica
51 Auction buy
52 Villain in Exodus
55 Response to a preacher
57 Tennis judge's cry
58 Entice W.W. II agents?
64 Racer Luyendyk
66 It's a fact
67 Site of the Taj Mahal
68 ___ suit (baggy outfit)
69 First name in cosmetics
70 "___ Over Beethoven"
71 Oscar winner Paquin
72 Takes five
73 Not just a five-minute jaunt

## DOWN

1 German industrial region
2 ___ podrida
3 Play around (with)
4 Dumbfound
5 "Mission: Impossible" assignment, maybe
6 Thought: Prefix
7 Screen pooch of 1939
8 Makes suds
9 Shortest light
10 Unimpressive brain size
11 Unplanned
12 Rock concert venue
13 Out of practice
21 End of a two-part move
22 Request before a click
26 Build
27 Shamu, for one
28 Rise quickly
29 Divvying-up process
31 Natural gas, for one
32 Common refrigerant
35 "___ Gantry"
37 Pac-10 team, for short
39 "Thank You" singer, 2001
40 Leave in a hurry
42 Steven Bochco series
43 Doesn't skimp with
48 Window smasher, maybe
50 Actors Begley and Begley Jr.
52 Public square
53 "Great white" bird
54 Preakness entrant
56 It's eye-grabbing
59 On the ___ (bickering)
60 Let stand, in editorial parlance
61 Aviation pioneer Sikorsky
62 ___ Stanley Gardner
63 Polio vaccine developer
65 LAX info

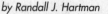

by Randall J. Hartman

# 62

## ACROSS

1 Puccini opera
6 Grasslands
10 Hole-making tool
13 "___ to Be You"
14 Laceless shoes
15 La-la lead-in
16 13
18 Obedience school command
19 Defensive tackle Warren ___
20 Suit to ___
21 Smallest postage hike
22 13
26 Abbreviate
28 Letter after epsilon
29 "Family Feud" host Anderson
30 Aim for many models
34 Abby's late sister
35 Bygone
37 Beyond tipsy
38 Hindmost brain parts
41 Rubbish
43 Rich soil
44 Side by side
46 13
50 "What's the ___?!"
51 Muzzleloader's load
52 Lacking thrills
55 "Scram!"
56 13
59 Bon ___
60 Like bustards and buzzards
61 One of the Muses
62 "Chasing ___" (1997 film)

63 Gravitate (toward)
64 Natural mimics

## DOWN

1 Diner jarful
2 Other, to Ortega
3 Stuck on board
4 Italian aperitif
5 Sidewalk stand drink
6 "Deathtrap" director
7 Misappropriate
8 How fans may go
9 Former Asian map abbr.
10 Perplexed
11 Dry with a twist
12 Morning eye-opener
14 Apply (for)

17 Dogtag info
21 Sleuth created by Biggers
23 Road sign abbr.
24 Thin blue line, say
25 It requires a PIN
26 Dis
27 Give an edge to
30 New Left org.
31 Controversial Oscar recipient of 1999
32 Tastes
33 "Never mind" to an editor
35 One of five Norwegian kings
36 Glove material
39 It connects to the elbow
40 Place to go in London?

41 Capote nickname
42 Parish residence
44 Gild
45 Some diner orders
46 Science society ___ Xi
47 Colorful phrase
48 Los Angeles attraction, with "the"
49 Leading
53 Prefix with tarsal
54 Grandson of Adam
56 Hanger-on?
57 Many a Monopoly property: Abbr.
58 Like L.B.J.

by Eric Berlin

## ACROSS

1 Old-time oath
5 Threaded fastener
10 Went out, as a fire
14 Auntie of Broadway
15 Fight site
16 Memo starter
17 Elvis's middle name
18 First line of a nursery rhyme
20 Creative guy
22 Make a goof
23 Matt of "Friends"
24 Delivery room doctors, for short
25 Hwy.
27 Symbol of slowness
28 Submarine sandwich
30 Colorado ski resort
31 Brother of Cain
33 Sign after Taurus
35 1961 Sinatra album
39 Divulge
40 He played Ricky on 50's TV
41 Took too much of a drug, briefly
42 Copycat
44 Japanese restaurant fare
49 "No ___" (Chinese menu phrase)
50 601, in old Rome
51 Place to play jai alai
53 Pamper
55 J. P. Morgan and others
56 Knocking sound
58 Cube inventor Rubik
59 Phoenix's state: Abbr.
60 Lab containers
61 Slippery part of a banana
62 Tennis great Sampras
63 White, to Latinos
64 Canvas bag

## DOWN

1 Sends a message by computer
2 Madison Square ___
3 One-celled protozoan
4 National park in Alaska
5 Brand of wrap
6 Chewed noisily
7 Soldier in Dixie
8 Fill with love
9 All-Star third baseman, 1985–96
10 Have ___ on (claim)
11 Five-time Tour de France winner Miguel
12 Ejecting lava
13 Cotillion girl
19 Battleship letters
21 Spanish province or its wine
26 Yale player
29 Omit in pronunciation
30 Rival school of The Citadel: Abbr.
32 Skier's headgear
34 The Wizard of Menlo Park
35 Old anti-Communist reaction
36 "Eureka!"
37 Actor Beatty
38 Spongelike toy
39 CD-___
43 Frisbee's inspiration, supposedly
45 Given away
46 Not mono
47 Big stinger
48 Shoe part
50 Banned insecticide
52 "Midnight Cowboy" character
54 Stupefy
56 Run-D.M.C.'s music
57 "You're it!" game

*by Peter Gordon*

# 64

## ACROSS
1 Nile slitherers
5 Masked critter
9 Expecting, as a raise
14 Opportunity, so to speak
15 Dagger handle
16 Monica of the courts
17 1999 Meryl Streep movie
20 "___ not fair!"
21 Gardener's need
22 Craving
23 Master's requirement, often
25 Met or Card, for short
27 Gateway Arch city: Abbr.
30 Midleg
32 Viands
34 Negative vote
36 Foolhardy
38 Interminably
39 Ayn Rand book
42 Out-and-out
43 Accordingly
44 Gives the nod
45 Ethel Waters classic
47 Fall shade
49 Twitch
50 Shows one's human side
52 Things with ___ (theme of this puzzle)
56 Yiddish plaints
57 Bread spread
59 Matterhorn, e.g.
60 1988 John Cleese movie, with "A"
65 Action spot
66 Easily molded
67 Bumped off
68 Fortuneteller's card
69 Golden rule word
70 Nothing more than

## DOWN
1 Own up to
2 Pole position?
3 Group that's rounded up
4 ___ Lanka
5 Picky people?
6 Meatheads
7 "Come here ___?"
8 Extreme
9 Leading down the aisle
10 Hammer part
11 It has many keys: Abbr.
12 Anthem preposition
13 Queue after Q
18 Goatee site
19 Gave the once-over
24 First U.S. space station
26 MacNeil's longtime news partner
27 Built for speed
28 Looks after
29 60's turn-on
31 Egg roll time
33 Colombia's capital
34 One of the Judds
35 Storage spot
37 "Quiet, please!"
40 Back street prowler
41 Not familiar with
42 Make lace
46 ___ Minor
48 Flat-bottomed boat
51 Wise lawgiver
53 Cyclist Armstrong
54 Respected one
55 Gardener's need
56 "It can't be!"
58 Took off
60 "___ chance!"
61 Lyrical Gershwin
62 Sun. talk
63 Baton Rouge sch.
64 Prepare to shoot

by Sherry O. Blackard

# 65

## ACROSS

1 ___ Lilly & Co.
4 Had creditors
8 Copier
14 Meld of the queen of spades and jack of diamonds
16 Some sorority women
17 Peruse?
18 Gets even with
19 Timeline segments
20 Chemin de ___
21 Lotion ingredient
22 Lith., formerly
23 Foreign exchange?
27 Takes a siesta
30 Touched down
31 Swimming (in)
33 "Believe it ___ . . ."
35 A founder of Dadaism
38 Beaten?
41 Oxford-to-London dir.
42 Simpleton
43 Job-specific vocabulary
44 Nut used to flavor Coke
45 Chip in
46 Atrophy?
51 Mathematician's degree?
54 In myth she was turned into a spring
55 Suffix with real
56 Ancient colonnade
57 Mere 1%, say
60 Shortstop?
62 Protective cover
63 Fix firmly in place
64 Plays the toady, perhaps
65 "The lady ___ protest . . ."
66 Sounds during doctor's exams

## DOWN

1 They might touch one's heart
2 Yarn makers
3 Personified
4 Columbus Day mo.
5 Quick smells
6 Bull in advertising
7 "Nothing runs like a ___"
8 Narrow sailing rte.
9 Compadre of Fidel
10 Buffet, e.g.
11 Author Calvino
12 Marshy inlet
13 Winding paths
15 Circus cries
24 Capital of ancient Lorraine
25 Flow stopper
26 His job is murder
28 Agent of Cleopatra's demise
29 Carbolic acid
31 Ripen
32 Horror maven Craven
33 At the break ___
34 Blushing
35 "Evita" setting
36 "Citizen Kane" studio
37 Winter hrs. in L.A.
39 Lady Macbeth, e.g.
40 Busts inside a museum
44 Rascally sorts
45 Best suited
46 Impertinent
47 Veil fabric
48 Natural athlete, supposedly
49 Named
50 "___ hooks" (box caution)
52 Spelunker's aid
53 Detests
56 HBO rival
58 Forbidden fruit partaker
59 In medias ___
61 Educ. institution

*by Jerry E. Rosman*

# 66

## ACROSS

1 Panorama
6 "I dare you!"
10 Meal-in-bed supporter
14 ___ and aahed
15 Upper hand
16 Hearty's companion
17 With 61-Across, a fictional pair who are hard to tell apart
19 Jane Austen heroine
20 Toward sunrise
21 Res ___ loquitur (legal phrase)
22 Face-valued, as stocks
23 Scurries
25 El ___ (Pacific phenomenon)
27 Family pair who are hard to tell apart
33 56-Across + 56-Across
34 For takeout
35 Enarmored of
36 Writer Wharton
38 "___ about that?!"
40 Hertz competitor
41 Satellite TV receivers
43 ___ is to say
45 Court subject
46 Routine that's hard to tell apart from past routines
49 "It's c-c-c-cold!"
50 Minipie
51 Laugh-filled
54 Prefix with potent
56 Fair share, maybe
60 Song for a diva
61 See 17-Across

63 Dovetail
64 Powerful auto engine
65 Remove from the blackboard
66 Feathery scarves
67 Shipped
68 So far

## DOWN

1 November catchword
2 Dubuque's state
3 The Rolling Stones' "___ a Rainbow"
4 Prepare to bite?
5 Say further
6 Sound that's heaved
7 Bookie's quote
8 Big lizard
9 Chairman pro ___

10 What a loser may throw in
11 Interstate entrance/exit
12 ___ mater
13 1776 or 1945
18 Deceive
22 Aardvark
24 On paper
26 Sort
27 Place for a sacred cow
28 Godly belief
29 Codgers
30 Counting everything
31 Wanderer
32 Frequent Arctic forecast
33 British refs.
37 Malaise
39 "And then . . . ?"

42 Popular camera type, for short
44 ". . . the way of a man with ___": Proverbs
47 Be half asleep
48 Not these or those
51 Window's support
52 Creme cookie
53 Actress Bonet
55 Lo ___ (noodle dish)
57 24 hours ___
58 ___-majesté
59 Centipede's multitude
61 Show showers
62 Pasture

by Manny Nosowsky

## ACROSS
1 Breathless state?
6 Bach's "Mass ___ Minor"
9 1930's French P.M. Léon
13 Dixie talk
14 ___-Day vitamins
15 Ambience
16 Record company
17 "Sense and Sensibility" actor, 1995
19 Altar vow
20 Works of Homer
22 Stimulate
23 1960's–70's pop singer/actor
26 ___ Wednesday
27 Dig in
28 Codebreakers' org.
31 Hectic episodes
34 Play starter
37 Most suitable
39 End of 17-, 23-, 50- or 61-Across
42 Severe lawgiver of Athens
43 Gave temporarily
44 Sticks up
45 Disney collector's item
46 Encyclopedia unit: Abbr.
48 Ground breaker
50 Rainbow Coalition founder
56 Signal enhancer
59 Confined, with "up"
60 "___ luck?"
61 "To Kill a Mockingbird" novelist
63 Welcome one's guests, maybe
65 Korea's home
66 Ogler
67 Family girl
68 In that case
69 Word of accord
70 English county bordering London

## DOWN
1 Go off script
2 Madrid museum
3 Mover and shaker
4 Lamb ma'am
5 Back streets
6 Occupied
7 Photo envelope enclosure, for short
8 Grand ___ (island near Florida)
9 Title for Münchhausen
10 Oahu wingding
11 Coffee holders
12 Chess ending
14 Cry of eagerness
18 Au ___ (how some potatoes are served)
21 "No way!"
24 Fundamental
25 Monarch's rule
28 Claudius I's successor
29 Swedish car
30 "___ Well That Ends Well"
31 Like some electric appliances
32 Potentially disastrous
33 Egg shape
35 Refs' decisions
36 Amount past due?
38 Shortstop Jeter
40 1956 Elvis hit
41 Filmmaker Coen
47 Fish hawk
49 Gas pump number
50 Sumo land
51 Blunt blades
52 Scoff (at)
53 "For goodness ___!"
54 In reserve
55 One of the original Baby Bells
56 First-rate, slangily
57 Skin problem
58 Cleveland's lake
62 Soapmaking need
64 Family girl

*by Ethan Cooper and Michael Shteyman*

# 68

## ACROSS

1 Brutish sort
6 Picture prize
11 Phone __
14 Vice president Stevenson
15 Seize, à la Caesar
16 Masseur's supply
17 Insect's bedtime ritual?
19 Bother
20 Hole-in-one
21 King in a Steve Martin song
22 1945 conference site
24 Part of a service
26 Perfumes with a joss stick, say
27 Induction motor developer
29 Very funny person
32 Game show panelist Peggy
35 Preschoolers
37 "__ Mio"
38 "Bleah!"
39 Sass from Elsie?
41 Shell mover
42 Ragú rival
44 Milton Friedman's subj.
45 Friend of Big Bird
46 __ Club
48 Dumbstruck
50 Hand down
52 Not stop for, in a way
56 Have in one's hands
58 Test site
59 Big D.C. lobby
60 Tick off
61 Sound when a gobbler gets a joke?
64 "Y" wearer
65 Actress Eleniak
66 Oscar-winning screenwriter Robert
67 Antonym's antonym: Abbr.
68 Knocks flat
69 Aligns

## DOWN

1 Raisin cakes
2 Bring out
3 Ragged Dick creator
4 Carrier to Copenhagen
5 Move quietly
6 One __ (ball game)
7 For example
8 Kind of sole
9 They have strings attached
10 Place to stretch your legs
11 Hammer for a hopper?
12 Disney musical
13 Latch (onto)
18 Totals
23 Tres y tres
25 Whitney and others: Abbr.
26 Puss's food container?
28 Game company that originated Yahtzee
30 Steamer, e.g.
31 Medal awardee, maybe
32 Putting targets
33 Prefix with cultural
34 Rams, lambs and ewes?
36 Move with difficulty
39 Dressed like a Victorian woman
40 Sort of
43 Fat, in France
45 Slippery sort
47 Make certain
49 Some beers
51 "Hamlet" courtier
53 Public, as information
54 Bucker
55 Director Peter
56 Bakers' wares
57 Alternative to De Gaulle
58 Pastoral places
62 Hateful org.
63 Today, in Toledo

*by Randolph Ross*

## ACROSS
1 Signs of healing
6 File folder parts
10 ___ of Capri
14 Apportion
15 Airline that serves only kosher food
16 Financial aid criterion
17 "Oh boy!"
18 Writer Ephron
19 Lotion ingredient
20 One whose name can be followed by "Esq.": Abbr.
21 Good-looking guy
23 Ho-hum
25 Sis's sib
26 W.W. II prison camp
29 China's most populous city
34 They replaced francs, marks and pesetas
35 Goatee's place
36 Hostel
37 Casual clothing item
41 Flow back
42 Business phone button
43 Nostalgic song
44 Big game on January 1
47 Portray
48 Pop's partner
49 Unwakable state
50 Easy-park shopping places
55 Dressed
59 Neighbor of Afghanistan
60 Egyptian queen, for short
61 Family girl

62 Vito Corleone's creator
63 Yard sale tag
64 Silly
65 Crystal ball gazer
66 Carrot on a snowman, perhaps
67 Card game that's a hint to today's theme

## DOWN
1 It's a long story
2 Coagulate
3 Plenty
4 Big hit?
5 Pork place?
6 Final frame for a bowler
7 Baseball's Moises
8 The ___ of Avon
9 Fast-paced, slangily

10 Dazed and confused
11 Prefix with defense and destruct
12 Fifth-century pope who was sainted
13 Adam's apple location?
21 Droop
22 Ornamental vase
24 Young woman
26 Passover meal
27 Sports car engine
28 Saudis, e.g.
29 Three-card monte assistant
30 Rear
31 Language in New Delhi
32 Prank
33 Atlas enlargement
35 Cornfield bird

38 Prominent shoe seller
39 Limerick, e.g.
40 "Scent of a Woman" star
45 Key of Tchaikovsky's Symphony No. 5
46 Fast-tempo jazz
47 Whoop-de-___ (big parties)
49 Tight-knit
50 Has a taste of, as wine
51 Test choice
52 Tear down
53 To boot
54 Luau necklaces
56 Plumbing problem
57 Pockmark cause
58 Bucks and does
61 Small bite

by Peter Gordon

## ACROSS

1 Sheep's cry
6 On ___ (like some jobs)
10 Subject of a Sophocles tragedy
14 Video's counterpart
15 Waterfront sight
16 Standard
17 Amorous entanglement
20 Discipline that uses koans
21 Send out
22 Member of a secret order
23 Eye opening for a squint
24 Sic a lawyer on
26 Annoyance for dwellers near airports
33 Bond's "Casino Royale" foe
34 Randomizer
35 Govt. initiative
36 Subsists (on)
37 Person with a chest pad
38 String section member
39 Possible solution
40 "Just ___ thought!"
41 Acted badly
42 Clothing label designation
45 Hertz offering
46 "Of all the luck!"
47 Posthumous donation
51 Actress Pitts of old films
52 Greetings
55 Mechanical impossibility
59 Nobelist Wiesel
60 Fairy tale opener

61 With 40-Down, seat of Orange County, Calif.
62 Wildcat
63 Jab
64 Readily available

## DOWN

1 Singer/activist Joan
2 Renaissance instrument
3 TV genie portrayer
4 Put on TV
5 Without inflection or feeling
6 Cheerleaders' finale, often
7 British P.M. under George III
8 Always with an apostrophe
9 Dernier ___

10 Ballet Russe star Pavlova
11 Helps, as a memory
12 Singer Guthrie
13 Marvel Comics group
18 Simple folk
19 "I agree completely!"
23 1996 horror film with sequels
24 Barbershop sound
25 Colorado native
26 Ammonia derivative
27 "Well, I ___!"
28 Campus offices: Abbr.
29 Thinks out loud
30 Fireplace tools
31 Treaded surfaces
32 "Good heavens!"
33 Boo-boo

37 Exploitative type
38 Musical artiste
40 See 61-Across
41 Fleeting muscle problem
43 Clearasil target
44 Irish port near Killarney
47 German automaker
48 Bank (on)
49 Alfred E. Neuman expression
50 Summit
51 "An Officer and a Gentleman" hero
52 Aid to the stumped
53 Smidgen
54 Say sharply
56 Blouse, e.g.
57 Game with "Draw Two" cards
58 Beachgoer's goal

*by Robert Malinow*

## ACROSS

1 Backs, anatomically
6 Plants
11 Bouncers' requests
14 Shackles
15 Like some anesthesia
16 Rolodex no.
17 With 31-, 46- and 61-Across, comment from Franz Kafka
19 Kidnappers in 70's news
20 Body build
21 Masterful
23 Online columnist Drudge
25 Abbr. on a business letter
28 "Would ___?"
29 Fugard's "A Lesson From ___"
31 See 17-Across
34 Off-the-cuff stuff
36 Butler's request
37 Ed.'s in-box filler
38 One using a delete key
40 Hesitation sound
43 Bother no end
44 City near Bologna
46 See 17-Across
50 Checks for contraband, maybe
51 Lash mark
52 Together, musically
54 Q.E.D. part
55 Counterpart of a delete key
58 Nervous feeling
60 Umpire's call
61 See 17-Across
66 Compete
67 For a specific purpose
68 Loo sign
69 Put the kibosh on
70 Time unit?
71 Picture within a picture

## DOWN

1 24 horas
2 Sun, e.g.
3 They may be pitched
4 Bull, at times
5 "___ silly question . . ."
6 Polished, languagewise
7 Part of U.C.L.A.
8 U.N. Day mo.
9 Broccoli ___ (leafy vegetable)
10 Football's Karras
11 ". . . is fear ___": F.D.R.
12 Texas border city
13 One working with heavy tiles
18 M.'s mate
22 Waterfront walk
23 Cripple
24 Poor-box filler
26 Bilked
27 Fast time?
30 Blip maker
32 Pion's place
33 Copy
35 Literally, "I forbid"
39 Strip in the news
40 Gives hope to
41 "Pure Moods" singer
42 It's rigged
43 Red-spotted critters
45 City on the Elbe
46 Jury, often
47 Self-referencing contract term
48 Walking on air
49 Subtle distinction
53 U.S.N.A. grad
56 Actor Morales
57 Cinergy Field players
59 Best Picture of 1958
62 Spa sounds
63 Marker letters
64 Western tribesman
65 One of a fleet fleet

*by David Levinson Wilk*

## ACROSS

1 Instruments at luaus
5 Island of Napoleon's exile
9 Was in the movies
14 Man with an ark
15 Harvest
16 Stage between egg and pupa
17 "Arsenic and Old Lace" star, 1944
19 Airedale, e.g., for dogs
20 Totally
21 Scottish miss
22 Electricians, at times
23 Creditor's demand
25 Numerous
26 Colony member
27 Japanese farewell
31 Demanding
34 Knee/ankle connector
35 Trojan War hero
36 Vehicle that's hailed
37 Astound
38 Capture
39 Song for a diva
40 Capitol feature
41 Ready to hit the sack
42 Shower accessories
44 Copacabana city
45 Manage
46 Gatherings where people hold hands
50 Horrified
53 Foreboding
54 Actress Gardner
55 Emergency light
56 "Liar Liar" star
58 Life of ___
59 Fix, as copy

60 Tricks
61 Follows the leader
62 One giving orders
63 Voice above bass

## DOWN

1 Open, as a bottle
2 Eucalyptus eater
3 Like the bird that catches the worm
4 Timid
5 Straying
6 Minimum
7 Outlaws
8 Fitting
9 Lacking pigment
10 Noted anti-alcohol crusader
11 Elder or alder
12 "As ___" (letter closing)
13 June honorees

18 Shuttle-riding senator
22 Oscar winner for "True Grit"
24 Top-selling vocalist of the 1990's
25 Corn
27 Phonies
28 A bit cracked?
29 Tool with teeth
30 Fired
31 Attempt
32 Skater Lipinski
33 Departure
34 Struck hard
37 Change according to circumstances
41 Crownlike headgear
43 Ambles
44 Does a double take, e.g.

46 Round after the quarters
47 "Deck the Halls," e.g.
48 Episode
49 Authority
50 Bushy do
51 Smooth-talking
52 Robust
53 Pal of Spot
56 One of the Bushes
57 Big TV maker

by Lynn Lempel

## ACROSS

1 Bit of street art
6 Taken wing
11 Toast topping
14 Japanese automaker
15 Part of a TV transmission
16 Have ___ at
17 Character actor in the Cowboy Hall of Fame
19 Modern: Prefix
20 Mandlikova of tennis
21 A.A.A. suggestion: Abbr.
22 Redecorate
24 Actress Long or Peeples
26 Jelly fruit
27 After-hours pool use, maybe
32 "Phooey!"
33 Regal headdresses
34 Social misfit
36 Pentium maker
38 Fivescore yrs.
39 Enter, as data
40 No longer working: Abbr.
41 Singer Twain
43 Number cruncher, for short
44 Boo-boo
47 Cultural values
48 Big inits. on the Net
49 Like a habanero pepper
51 Nabokov novel
53 Agenda, for short
57 Dory need
58 Panhandler's request
61 Joanne of "Abie's Irish Rose"

62 Guys' prom attire, informally
63 Continental divide?
64 Shade tree
65 Minute ___ (thin cut)
66 Down and out

## DOWN

1 Moonshiner's mixture
2 Bruins' sch.
3 Totally trash
4 Cardin rival
5 Pool distance
6 It's the truth
7 Gospel writer
8 Poetic homage
9 They start pitches
10 "Uh-uh!"
11 15th-century Flemish painter

12 Pulitzer winner James
13 Drop anchor
18 Farsi speaker
23 Like Dolly the clone
25 Part of IHOP: Abbr.
26 Designer Versace
27 Trig figures
28 Orchestra percussion
29 Pleasure craft
30 Most of "The Wizard of Oz"
31 Be crabby
32 Cone bearer
35 Kind of "fingerprint"
37 Designer Head
39 Green Hornet's sidekick
41 Decathlon event
42 Stern or Hayes

45 Halloween characters
46 ___-Lorraine
49 Took a tram, e.g.
50 James ___ Carter
51 Square mileage
52 Place to work
54 "Trick" joint
55 Dated expletive
56 Refuse
59 Woodcutter's tool
60 Snookums

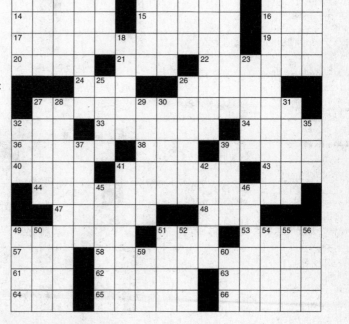

by Bob Peoples

# 74

## ACROSS
1 Kingdom east of Fiji
6 Sea plea
9 "If I ___ rich man . . ."
14 Like some suspects
15 Doll's name
16 Summing up
17 Hose part
18 Roll call call
19 See 11-Down
20 Faster than moderato
22 Not so vigorous
24 Spotted
25 "This ___" (carton label)
27 Carnival follower
28 "___ Is Born"
30 Tick off
32 Writers' references
35 Capsular, biologically
39 CARE packages, say
40 Emotionally burned out
42 Prefix with meter
43 Show shame
45 Grid official
47 Play for a sap
48 ___ nous
49 One teaspoon, maybe
52 Natural skyline former
54 Unwanted cyber-ads
58 Most villainous
60 Rubout
62 Not just sip
63 Blow it
65 Fail miserably
66 ___ wrench
67 Partner of Larry and Curly
68 Everything, to Einstein
69 In sorry shape
70 Landscaper's supply
71 Ebbets Field hero

## DOWN
1 Yellowfin and bluefin
2 "___ Mio"
3 Loving motion
4 Lead ores
5 "Break ___!"
6 1957 Marlon Brando film
7 "The loneliest number"
8 Screw-up
9 Off the mark
10 Gives power to
11 With 19-Across, flashy display
12 Former ABC sitcom
13 On the ball
21 Many 12/26 store visitors
23 Focal point
26 By no means poured
29 Things to crack
31 Actress Winona
32 Old-time punishment need
33 Get a move on
34 Announcer Hall
36 Aunt Polly's nephew
37 Cretan peak
38 Bamboozle
41 Didn't go away
44 Fought it out, in Britain
46 Permanently attached, to a zoologist
49 Painter of ballerinas
50 Fertilization site
51 Steakhouse sound
53 Agenda entries
55 This is one
56 Van Gogh's "Bedroom at ___"
57 Reagan attorney general
59 Chooser's start
61 Off yonder
64 Kanga's kid

by Joel Kaplow

## ACROSS

1 Furrowed part of the head
5 Cougars
10 Door fastener
14 "The ___ Ranger"
15 Basketball Hall-of-Famer Thomas
16 Hitch, as oxen
17 Start of a free call
20 "___, humbug!"
21 Hair removal brand
22 Not stand steadily
23 New York's ___ Place
25 Letter before omega
26 From ___ Z
27 Switzerland's Zug or Zurich
29 Hammer and mallet
31 Conclude by
32 "To thine own ___ be true"
33 Pepsi rival
37 1943 Mary Martin musical
40 Marquis de ___
41 Turndowns
42 Like some gases
43 Move crabwise
45 Shrewd
46 "Mamma ___!"
49 El ___ (Spanish hero)
50 Not stale, as chips
51 "O Canada," e.g.
53 Dear one, in Italy
54 Split ___ with ham
57 Some gamblers' weaknesses
60 Like books
61 A Brontë sister
62 Burden
63 "My Friend" of old radio
64 Pacifists
65 Opposed to, in "Li'l Abner"

## DOWN

1 1950's horror film creature, with "the"
2 Writer Jaffe
3 Like some baseball catches
4 Tiny
5 Easy mark, slangily
6 Theater worker
7 Baseball glove
8 "How nice!"
9 Stops, as electricity
10 Jekyll's counterpart
11 Cardiologist's concern
12 ___ shooting
13 California's San ___ Bay
18 Completely
19 Astronaut Armstrong
24 Roll call at a political convention
25 Some casual shirts
27 Corporate honchos, for short
28 The "I" of "The King and I"
29 Giggle
30 Perfumes
32 Bawl out
34 Getting ahead of
35 Composer Weill
36 Villa d' ___
38 Strong as always
39 Optometrist's concern
44 Bakery worker
45 Layouts
46 New Zealand native
47 Kind of tube or ear
48 1980's George Peppard series, with "The"
50 The "C" of CNN
52 "Mary ___ little lamb"
53 404, in old Rome
55 Carrier for needles and pins
56 Org.
58 Comedian Philips
59 ___ double take

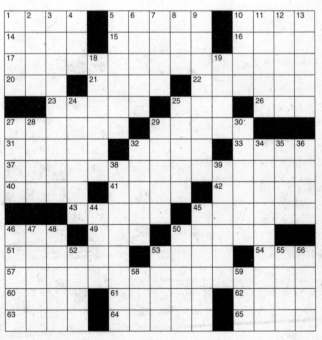

by Charles E. Gersch

# 1

```
A D M S    S P A S M    Z A N Y
B R I O    H E L L O    A L O E
Y A L U    E P C O T    P E W S
S M A R T A S A W H I P
M A N D A R I N      S A L S A
      O R S      L O U    A O L
E T T U      N I E T Z S C H E
B R I G H T A S A B U T T O N
B I G H E A D E D      R O T E
E T H    A B A      U S E
D E T A T      A P P L E P I E
      S H A R P A S A T A C K
J I M I    L E I G H    C L I I
A R E A    M I N E O    A M A N
B E A N    A N G S T    R A N G
```

# 2

```
E A S T    S W A M P    S T A B
R U L E    L A K E R    T A X I
E G A N    A R I S E    A C I D
C U T D O W N T O S I G H S
T R Y O N      A N S A
      N E V E      M A N N A
L E T    B A T T H E B R I E S
A Q U A    S C R O D    K N O T
P U R P L E H A Y E S    E N O
P I N T O      A N E W
      E D A M      G A S P E
      T H E W I Z A R D O F A H S
J A I L    T U N E R    E D I T
U C L A    C R O N E    R I L E
G O O N    H E R O D    S E E R
```

# 3

```
Z E T A    B U N T    A R G O T
I V A N    O N C E    G E O D E
N E X T    S T O R A G E B I N
C R I S I S I S I S I S I N
      B E E      T E E
A C R O S S    O O H S    R A M
T R I K E    S H I M    P O T S
B A N A N A N A N A N A M E D
A N D Y    P A R K    E I E I O
Y E S    P I P E    S A L O N S
      S H E      L E T
   R O C O C O C O C O C O P Y
S E N A T E R A C E    O H I O
I N T R O    B R A D    O N L Y
R O O F S    S A L E    P O L O
```

# 4

```
M A R C    E W E S    H E M E N
A L O U    C H I C    O R A T E
S E A R    H E R A    M I N C E
S U N F L O W E R S E E D
A T S E A      A I R    I L E
      W H A L E B L U B B E R
L E B    R U I N    N O L A N
E L L A    F E D U P    N E S S
A L A N S    O A T S    S E T
P I C T U R E F R A M E
T S K    P U N    E N S U E
      H U R R I C A N E L A M P
P R O S E    G O B I    A B B E
S A L E M    M A L L    C O R E
S W E D E    A L E E    E T A S
```

# 5

```
B L O C    B E E T S    M E T A
R I V A    R E G A L    A N O N
A T E M P O R A R Y    Y E G G
G E R S H W I N    C O R A L
      O N E    A M B R O S E
S C O O T S    A W E S
P O R N O    I N A N    T E A M
I N S A N I T Y C U R A B L E
N E O N    T A O S    E D A M S
      S E L F    B W A N A S
A C A D E M Y    F I E
Z A I R E    O L E A N D E R
T I M E    B Y M A R R I A G E
E R A S    M A N I C    T H I N
C O T S    W H I L E    E L S E
```

## 6

```
C A S T █ █ T A R █ E R S E
A R T E █ A G A P E █ R E L Y
C O A X █ D E C A L █ A J A R
T U R A N D O T C O M █ O P E
U N E S C O █ █ H A N O I █ █
S D S █ O N T H E D O T C O M
█ █ S T A Y █ █ P I E T A █ █
D A M P █ O P A L S █ C R O P
I S A A C █ █ T A T A █ █ █ █
M I C R O D O T C O M █ A P U
█ A K R O N █ █ O M E L E T █
B A R █ P O L K A D O T C O M
A R O N █ D I E G O █ H O R O
J A N E █ A N I O N █ O T I S
A L I T █ D E R █ █ S T A T █
```

## 7

```
T O W E L █ M A T E R █ A D S
E M I L Y █ A S I D E █ V E T
T A L K I N G H E A D █ E V A
E N D █ N O P E █ █ H O N O R
█ █ W A G G I N G T O N G U E
O P E N T O E █ L A T T E R █
P E S T O █ J A M S █ █ █ █ █
E A T S █ D I O D E █ C H O W
█ █ █ P A R E █ █ W H E R E █
█ P A Y O L A █ S P R E A D S
C H E A T I N G H E A R T █ █
H A R P S █ A E O N █ W O E █
A S A █ H E L P I N G H A N D
P E T █ O R I E L █ L A V E D
S S E █ T E T R A █ E L E G Y
```

## 8

```
P E D S █ L E T B E █ F R A N
E L I A █ A V E R S █ R A G A
E V E N █ N I N E T E E N T H
W I L D W I L D W E S T █ █ █
E R A S E █ █ S E P █ T O O █
E A U █ G R A Y █ M Y O H M Y
█ G L O A T E R █ R I I S █ █
█ W H A T W O M E N W A N T █
T H I N █ M E N F O L K █ █ █
A E N E A S █ N O L O █ S O T
M T G █ W P A █ █ E N T R Y █
█ █ W O R L D W I D E W E B █
J U B I L A T I O N █ G I G A
A G O G █ N E C K S █ E C O L
W H Y S █ G R E E T █ V E N T
```

## 9

```
W A G S █ R A M P █ R E A P
E T U I █ S O N I A █ E R G O
E R M A █ C O E D S █ D I E T
D I M M E R S W I T C H E S █
S A Y █ V A T █ █ R O O █ █ █
█ █ █ A I M █ B L A S T O F F
O H A R A █ D R A M █ █ S E E
S E V E N Y E A R I T C H E S
L E I █ █ A L I D █ O R A L S
O L D W O R L D █ N A Y █ █ █
█ █ I N D █ S O S █ A G A █
█ S I D E A R M P I T C H E S
B A B E █ R O A R S █ H O N K
O V E N █ M O R A Y █ A M I E
W E T S █ S T E T █ █ R E E D
```

## 10

```
C A P P █ M E G A █ J A M E S
A L E E █ A L A S █ A G E N T
P I N K S L I P S █ N E R D Y
█ █ N O E L █ A N I █ C U E █
M E Y E R █ S I D E T R I P S
A M A █ S T U N █ W O O █ █ █
S A N E █ I N S █ D R O N E █
H I T T I N G T H E S K I D S
█ L E N N Y █ Y M A █ S C I S
█ █ A F T █ L O L A █ E F T █
M U D S L I D E S █ S O N Y S
O N O █ A M I █ █ G O N E █
S C R A M █ T W I N F A L L S
E L I T E █ S O D A █ I L E S
S E C T S █ Y E O W █ R Y A N
```

## 11

```
ALFA BANS  SLOPE
ROAN ALOE  TATER
ABUT NEAR  UTTER
BOXINGCHAMPION
     TOO   EON
HAIRTRIGGER  CAB
ARGUE MOLT BARR
CELS APRES AIRE
KNOT VEGA  ARRAS
SAO  TALENTSCOUT
      LEI  ATE
 STERLINGSILVER
SHEAR MEAT OILY
RUSSO PALE NOSE
INTER SPAR ALES
```

## 12

```
GRUBS ELKS  ACTS
RUNAT NOAH  CHOP
UNCLE TOTO  AURA
BALLPARK  OLDMAN
STEP  LEI   TAI
    ALIENS  BASIC
ENTREE TIS   ERA
LOOKINTHEMIRROR
KAT   SIE  OCEANS
SHOOT  SMOKED
     LAB ICE LAWS
ACADIA  REDLIGHT
CHUM SERA  AGGIE
TORA IRON  WHITE
SPAN CARS  STEEP
```

## 13

```
MESA  HOPS  SERA
ORAL BEFRIENDED
PASTPERFORMANCE
 SHELLS    SPATE
      ROO TDS USSR
PONE WIRETAP
LUIGI NOBEL  ARM
ISNOTAGUARANTEE
ETA SNOBS  ROTOR
    PANTLEG  NYSE
ALTO ESE   LIE
LOOPS    TENSES
OFFUTURERESULTS
STUPENDOUS  CLAD
SSSS  ESSE  HATS
```

## 14

```
FRED OLES  GAYER
LOGO LIRA  REEVE
ADAM ELIS  ESSEX
RADICALCHICO
ENSNARE   NOPETS
    IVY WET SPIN
PEACE SIRED ITO
OSCARTHEGROUCHO
UTE SOULS  ONSET
TOLD RED   ADS
SPARKS  DNATEST
 AEOLIANHARPO
GROWL ANNE  BRED
NEILL INCA  LOLA
PALSY NOEL  ELLY
```

## 15

```
BEAD GASP  GATOR
ERGO ACHE  AFIRE
AMEN LIAR  ZONED
MINNIEDRIVER
UNDER  ISABELLA
PEA VIE CLOSETS
    RIALTO  AIDS
  MINNEAPOLIS
ABCS  CREWED
SICKEST SET FOE
POLYMERS  UTURN
  MINICOMPUTER
SPOOL CAPO  RIGA
LEAVE ALTO  FLOP
YIKES LEST  SENT
```

# 16

| S | A | S | S | | | S | P | R | E | E | | | A | L | G | A |
| T | R | E | K | | | P | R | O | A | M | | | M | O | R | T |
| A | L | L | Y | | | R | I | P | U | P | | | I | G | O | R |
| G | O | L | D | M | I | N | E | | | L | U | G | O | S | I | |
| | | | | I | M | E | T | | | B | O | N | A | N | Z | A |
| G | O | O | V | E | R | | | M | A | Y | A | S | | | | |
| A | N | N | E | | | E | A | T | E | R | | | G | R | R | |
| Y | O | U | R | E | I | N | T | H | E | M | O | N | E | Y | |
| E | R | S | | | G | N | A | T | S | | | P | A | P | A | |
| | | | S | Y | N | C | S | | | D | R | E | W | O | N | |
| J | A | C | K | P | O | T | | | R | A | I | N | | | | |
| A | R | N | E | T | T | | | W | I | N | D | F | A | L | L | |
| M | E | O | W | | | I | R | O | N | S | | | I | S | E | E |
| B | E | T | E | | | M | A | N | G | O | | | R | I | F | T |
| S | L | E | D | | | E | G | G | O | N | | | E | F | T | S |

# 17

| S | P | I | T | | | O | F | F | E | R | | | S | M | U | T |
| H | E | R | E | | | S | E | L | M | A | | | O | A | T | H |
| O | R | A | N | G | E | S | U | B | M | A | R | I | N | E | |
| D | U | N | N | O | | | S | E | L | E | C | T | M | E | N | |
| | | | | I | D | L | E | | | E | N | E | | | | |
| J | A | R | S | | | I | D | E | M | | | T | O | M | E | S |
| A | C | E | | | P | O | U | T | | | S | A | L | O | M | E |
| B | O | S | T | O | N | P | U | R | P | L | E | S | O | X | |
| B | R | A | V | O | S | | | D | E | I | S | | | E | T | E |
| A | N | W | A | R | | | D | E | C | K | | | S | L | E | D |
| | | | | M | M | I | | | A | E | O | N | | | | |
| A | P | P | R | A | I | S | E | R | | | R | O | U | S | E | |
| G | R | E | E | N | C | H | I | P | S | T | O | C | K | S | |
| R | O | L | E | | | R | E | N | E | S | | | P | L | A | N |
| A | P | E | D | | | O | D | E | T | S | | | S | A | T | E |

# 18

| S | A | L | E | M | | | A | L | D | A | | | E | T | T | A |
| E | L | O | P | E | | | R | U | I | N | | | L | I | E | N |
| W | A | I | S | T | M | A | N | A | G | E | M | E | N | T | |
| S | E | N | O | R | A | | | A | L | E | X | | | U | S | E |
| | | | M | I | L | E | R | | | L | O | P | P | E | D | |
| T | A | M | | | C | A | T | | | M | A | T | E | | | |
| O | R | E | M | | | W | H | O | A | | | I | N | A | N | E |
| M | I | N | E | R | I | N | F | R | A | C | T | I | O | N | |
| S | A | U | D | I | | | I | T | C | H | | | A | R | N | O |
| | | | E | P | I | C | | | I | O | N | | | Y | E | S |
| S | C | R | A | P | S | | | M | A | R | I | E | | | | |
| A | R | E | | | L | O | S | E | | | S | K | A | T | E | S |
| H | O | S | T | E | L | T | A | K | E | O | V | E | R | S | |
| I | N | T | O | | | D | O | N | E | | | L | E | A | S | T |
| B | E | S | T | | | E | A | S | Y | | | A | S | S | E | S |

# 19

| G | R | A | S | P | | | P | E | L | F | | | M | A | M | A |
| S | A | N | T | A | | | A | P | E | R | | | A | L | E | X |
| A | N | N | U | L | | | W | I | N | E | | | M | I | R | E |
| | | | | B | O | U | N | C | I | N | G | B | A | L | L | |
| O | R | B | | | M | T | S | | | E | R | A | S | E | S | |
| B | O | O | K | I | E | | | B | I | T | E | | | | | |
| E | D | W | I | N | | | T | A | T | I | | | E | M | M | A |
| Y | E | L | L | O | W | B | R | I | C | K | R | O | A | D | |
| S | O | S | O | | | E | A | T | S | | | I | R | A | T | E |
| | | | | S | T | R | S | | | I | N | S | T | E | P | |
| C | A | L | A | I | S | | | L | T | D | | | S | O | T | |
| I | N | S | T | R | U | C | T | I | O | N | S | | | | |
| V | I | A | L | | | I | R | O | N | | | E | N | A | C | T |
| E | S | T | A | | | T | O | N | E | | | S | I | N | A | I |
| T | E | S | S | | | S | P | I | N | | | S | P | A | R | E |

# 20

| F | A | K | E | | | L | A | M | B | S | | | F | U | M | E |
| A | R | A | L | | | A | N | N | I | E | | | I | B | A | R |
| T | U | R | K | E | Y | T | O | R | T | | | D | E | L | I | |
| A | B | A | | | V | E | E | | | C | O | T | E | R | I | E |
| L | A | T | H | E | R | | | C | H | U | R | L | | | | |
| | | | E | R | I | C | A | | | T | I | C | K | L | E | |
| D | I | A | L | | | N | U | T | S | | | M | A | N | I | A |
| A | C | R | E | | | G | R | E | E | R | | | S | E | A | R |
| M | E | A | N | S | | | T | R | E | E | | | T | E | R | N |
| P | T | B | O | A | T | | | E | R | A | T | O | | | | |
| | | | F | L | O | O | D | | | S | E | R | A | P | E | |
| F | L | A | T | T | O | P | | | D | O | N | | | G | O | D |
| L | O | G | O | | | L | E | M | O | N | D | O | R | P | S | |
| A | L | A | R | | | E | R | A | S | E | | | P | E | P | E |
| W | A | R | Y | | | D | A | T | E | R | | | T | E | A | L |

## 21

```
W O O D   P E W S   B O Z O S
O H N O   O X E N   A T A R I
M I L E   L U L U   M O N E T
B O Y S W I L L B E B O Y S
      T A C T     A I L
A D M I R E   A D S   E S P N
C R A M S   S L E E P   T O E
H O P E A G A I N S T H O P E
O W L   W A G E S   B A R E D
O N E S   M A N   F O L K S Y
    A T M     G R A F
  L I V E A N D L E T L I V E
C O R A L   C E O S   I D E A
U S A G E   A L A N   F L A T
E S S E X   A L T O   E E L S
```

## 22

```
W A T T   A S T I R   A V I D
E M E R   V E R N E   S A N E
B O X I N G R I N G   A C N E
T R A C E   B O E R   R A S P
V E N E E R   R E R U N
      P R O A M   T I L T E D
T A B S   T H O M   C E L L O
A M I   I C E P A C K   O S U
C E L L S   M U L L   S T A R
O N L O A N   P I E T A
    Y O Y O S   F I N A L E
S I C K   P A C T   E D W I N
P A L S   R U B B E R B A N D
A G U E   O N E A L   A R E A
R O B E   B A R R Y   G E N T
```

## 23

```
F E A T   E L M O   S P O O K
A C R E   N E A R   P U R G E
I R E S   T A T E   E N O L A
R U S S I A N H O M E   N E T
      M I T   A C T O R S
C O R R A L   R I C H E
A M E E R   S O R A   E D G E
F I N N I S H Y O U R M E A L
E T T E   M E A N   H E A L S
    G R I L L   M I D D L E
R E P E A T   T O N
I L E   T H A I B R E A K E R
S E T A T   B R I O   R A V E
K N E L L   B A R N   A L E E
S A R G E   E N D S   L E N D
```

## 24

```
R O B S   T R A S H Y   A L F
O S L O   S U B L E T   G E L
T H U N D E R R O A D   I V E
S A R G E   A P R   A L E E
      S E S A M E S T R E E T
P T A   M E R   T A R
A A R P   C U P S   P I E T A
S U N S E T B O U L E V A R D
S T E A M   A L M A   E R I E
    L I P   U V A   L O N
P R I M R O S E P A T H
E O N S   L A X   T I B E T
A G O   T I N P A N A L L E Y
R U N   O C T O P I   L A R K
L E E   W E A S E L   S H O E
```

## 25

```
L A R U E   T A M P A   Q U M
A R E N A   A L I A R   U N A
N E P L U S U L T R A   I C H
E S S O   I T S   C R A D L E
      C H E   S H A R P E R
B A S K E T S   P E T E R
A M I   R E W A R D   S O W N
R I N S E   E R A   T O Q U E
T R E K   L A T I N I   U S A
    Q U I E T   N E T C O S T
T R U A N T S   G O O
R O A S T S   O U R   S I T E
U S N   A D I N F I N I T U M
C I O   C I S C O   I N E R T
K E N   T E T E S   P E R K S
```

## 26

| A | I | O | L | I | ■ | L | O | D | E | ■ | F | E | T | A |
|---|---|---|---|---|---|---|---|---|---|---|---|---|---|---|
| S | O | N | I | C | ■ | A | M | E | X | ■ | A | L | A | N |
| S | W | I | P | E | A | D | E | B | I | T | C | A | R | D |
| N | A | T | ■ | B | R | U | N | ■ | T | E | E | N | S | Y |
| ■ | ■ | S | A | C | K | ■ | T | V | A | D | ■ | ■ | ■ | ■ |
| L | I | F | T | T | H | E | V | E | I | L | ■ | S | R | A |
| A | L | E | P | H | ■ | E | R | S | ■ | A | M | A | N | ■ |
| Z | E | T | A | ■ | M | E | D | I | A | ■ | N | E | J | D |
| A | N | E | T | ■ | A | R | I | ■ | O | N | A | I | R | ■ |
| R | E | D | ■ | P | I | N | C | H | A | N | E | R | V | E |
| ■ | ■ | C | O | N | E | ■ | A | L | E | X | ■ | ■ | ■ | ■ |
| A | S | T | R | O | S | ■ | M | P | A | A | ■ | Q | E | D |
| S | T | E | A | L | T | H | E | P | I | C | T | U | R | E |
| S | I | T | Z | ■ | E | M | M | E | ■ | T | R | I | T | E |
| T | R | E | Y | ■ | M | O | O | N | ■ | S | I | Z | E | D |

## 27

| A | T | A | R | I | ■ | S | N | I | P | ■ | L | U | S | H |
|---|---|---|---|---|---|---|---|---|---|---|---|---|---|---|
| R | O | B | I | N | ■ | T | A | D | A | ■ | A | R | E | A |
| K | N | U | C | K | L | E | S | A | N | D | W | I | C | H |
| S | I | T | E | ■ | E | P | A | ■ | T | R | Y | S | T | S |
| ■ | ■ | ■ | ■ | C | O | M | O | ■ | W | H | E | E | ■ | ■ |
| ■ | S | L | A | P | O | N | T | H | E | W | R | I | S | T |
| S | P | O | K | E | N | ■ | H | E | R | ■ | ■ | N | C | O |
| T | I | R | E | D | ■ | J | E | T | ■ | A | S | T | R | O |
| A | C | E | ■ | O | A | T | ■ | C | L | A | R | E | T | ■ |
| B | E | N | D | I | N | G | A | N | E | L | B | O | W | ■ |
| ■ | ■ | I | D | O | S | ■ | E | L | S | E | ■ | ■ | ■ | ■ |
| P | A | R | L | O | R | ■ | A | T | L | ■ | R | E | N | T |
| S | H | O | U | L | D | E | R | H | O | L | S | T | E | R |
| S | O | O | T | ■ | E | R | I | E | ■ | P | A | R | E | E |
| T | Y | K | E | ■ | R | E | A | R | ■ | S | W | E | D | E |

## 28

| B | E | T | S | ■ | P | A | P | A | S | ■ | G | R | I | P |
|---|---|---|---|---|---|---|---|---|---|---|---|---|---|---|
| M | A | U | I | ■ | A | T | O | N | E | ■ | R | E | N | E |
| T | U | R | N | S | L | O | O | S | E | ■ | A | N | T | E |
| ■ | A | C | O | M | P | L | E | T | E | F | O | O | L | ■ |
| A | N | N | E | X | ■ | L | O | X | ■ | I | N | S | ■ | ■ |
| R | O | D | ■ | F | O | R | M | ■ | H | A | R | E | ■ | ■ |
| C | R | O | S | S | E | Y | E | ■ | T | A | B | ■ | ■ | ■ |
| ■ | A | T | O | T | A | L | F | A | I | L | U | R | E | ■ |
| ■ | ■ | A | P | T | ■ | E | T | C | E | T | E | R | A | ■ |
| ■ | P | I | K | A | ■ | A | R | E | S | ■ | A | I | R | ■ |
| R | O | B | ■ | U | L | M | ■ | ■ | I | S | L | E | T | ■ |
| A | M | I | L | L | I | O | N | B | U | C | K | S | ■ | ■ |
| J | E | S | U | ■ | B | R | I | A | N | K | E | I | T | H |
| A | L | E | X | ■ | R | A | N | T | O | ■ | E | Z | R | A |
| H | O | S | E | ■ | A | L | O | S | S | ■ | T | E | A | L |

## 29

| S | O | D | A | S | ■ | T | E | N | A | M | ■ | A | H | S |
|---|---|---|---|---|---|---|---|---|---|---|---|---|---|---|
| C | N | O | T | E | ■ | E | X | I | L | E | ■ | H | I | T |
| A | C | O | R | N | F | L | A | K | E | S | ■ | E | N | E |
| R | E | D | E | A | L | ■ | M | E | X | ■ | D | A | D | E |
| ■ | ■ | ■ | S | T | A | R | ■ | S | I | Z | E | D | U | P |
| C | R | A | T | E | R | E | D | ■ | S | E | N | D | ■ | ■ |
| O | U | T | ■ | S | E | T | I | N | ■ | N | E | R | D | S |
| S | T | O | W | ■ | D | I | V | O | T | ■ | B | E | E | T |
| I | S | L | A | M | ■ | P | A | R | O | L | ■ | S | M | U |
| ■ | L | I | E | D | ■ | S | T | R | A | P | S | I | N | ■ |
| B | O | B | S | L | E | D | ■ | H | O | P | E | ■ | ■ | ■ |
| A | L | O | T | ■ | A | R | T | ■ | I | D | E | A | L | S |
| L | E | O | ■ | A | R | O | M | A | D | O | W | N | E | Y |
| S | O | T | ■ | F | I | N | E | D | ■ | G | E | T | O | N |
| A | S | H | ■ | T | E | E | N | S | ■ | S | E | I | N | E |

## 30

| F | I | L | C | H | ■ | A | R | E | S | ■ | T | H | I | N |
|---|---|---|---|---|---|---|---|---|---|---|---|---|---|---|
| L | O | I | R | E | ■ | G | U | R | U | ■ | W | A | C | O |
| A | T | L | A | S | ■ | A | T | T | N | ■ | O | L | E | S |
| B | A | T | S | I | N | T | H | E | B | E | L | F | R | Y |
| ■ | ■ | ■ | S | T | I | E | S | ■ | A | M | I | ■ | ■ | ■ |
| H | U | T | ■ | A | B | S | ■ | S | T | U | T | T | E | R |
| A | L | I | S | T | ■ | ■ | I | C | H | ■ | E | R | N | O |
| S | N | A | K | E | I | N | T | H | E | G | R | A | S | S |
| N | A | R | Y | ■ | S | E | E | ■ | ■ | I | S | S | U | E |
| T | R | A | L | A | L | A | ■ | S | A | N | ■ | H | E | S |
| ■ | ■ | I | R | A | ■ | A | M | I | G | O | ■ | ■ | ■ | ■ |
| F | R | O | G | I | N | T | H | E | T | H | R | O | A | T |
| O | A | T | H | ■ | D | U | E | L | ■ | A | N | K | L | E |
| G | R | I | T | ■ | E | T | A | L | ■ | M | O | R | O | N |
| S | A | S | S | ■ | R | U | D | Y | ■ | S | T | A | T | S |

## 31

```
L I L A C █ P A L E █ M E A T
O D O U R █ R E A L █ E L L A
C O C K A D O O D L E D O O M
I L K █ T E N N █ S N I P E S
█ S P E N T █ █ █ I C E S █
M A M A █ T O P D O G S █ █
E R I C A █ █ H A R M █ F R O
L I T T L E K A N G A R O O M
D A H █ L E I S █ S A U T E █
█ █ B O L D E S T █ I R O N
█ S H I V █ █ T E L L S █ █
A P O G E E █ S E R A █ C S A
C E N T R A L P A R K Z O O M
M A K O █ R E A M █ E E R I E
E R S E █ N A R Y █ R E E L S
```

## 32

```
I M P A L E █ L A N G █ S E R
T O O L E R █ A P E R █ H O I
S O L O N S █ C L E O █ A L B
█ █ I H A T E T O R U S S I A
A T T A █ █ R O M █ N A T A L
L E I █ V O W █ B A D H A N D
E S C █ O V I D █ M C I █ █
█ H O W C A N I S E R B I A █
█ O A T █ G I B E █ C U D █
H U R T L E D █ S A W █ E R A
E N I A C █ E T A █ █ S W A Y
I D O N O T B O L I V I A █
N U T █ R O A N █ B I G T O P
I L E █ D O S E █ I N H E R E
E L D █ S K E D █ D E T R O P
```

## 33

```
A S I S █ A T O Z █ C R A B S
C O M P █ R O P E █ H A R E M
C H A I N M A I L █ A C U T E
T O M E I █ D U D █ R E B E L
█ █ █ G N P █ M A I L C A L L
N I C E T R Y █ S E A █ █
C A L L H O M E █ T Y R A N T
A G A █ █ B A T C H █ T E A
R O M A N O █ H O M E L O A N
█ █ M E N █ M U T A N T S █
L O A N W O R D █ S H U █ █
E R R E D █ A R E █ I G L O O
A B U S E █ W O R D C H A I N
V I S T A █ L O G O █ I D L E
E T H Y L █ S P O T █ N E S S
```

## 34

```
A C N E █ T E A S █ O S C A R
D O E R █ R A V I █ S P O R E
I M P S █ A R I Z █ T A L K S
D E A T H I N V E N I C E █ █
A T L █ O P S █ C A E S A R
S H I R R S █ J A R █ L T D
█ I R E F U L █ I P A N A █
█ D I V I D I N G I N T W O █
W I N E D █ S T A N C E █ █
S E C █ A H A █ N U R S E S
J U L I U S █ F O B █ M I A
█ I N T H E V I C I N I T Y
D O N U T █ D A N E █ E T H S
I S E R E █ A L A N █ W H E N
S E D E R █ M E L T █ T Y R O
```

## 35

```
A R M S █ F O S S E █ L P G A
L O O M █ A V I A N █ I R A N
T A R O T C A R D S █ Z O R A
A R A R A T █ A U K █ T A L
R E S E W █ A S T R O L O G Y
S D S █ D E B T █ E D U C E S
█ █ C R I E R S █ L O S T
█ C R Y S T A L B A L L █
O P I E █ S N O O P S █ █
U R G E O N █ G E N L █ D O R
T E A L E A V E S █ O F E V E
A P R █ N B A █ E M O T E D
G A B S █ O U I J A B O A R D
E R O O █ B L O A T █ L I D O
S E X Y █ S T U B S █ S L O G
```

## 36

```
HEARD  BUBBA  MBA
ALBEE  AREAS  RUN
MISSMANNERS  BET
   PUPAS  BATONS
ADMIRAL  BLUEJAY
SORTER  PAELLA
INKER  WORST  NIA
DUNS  PIPES  AGTS
ETO  PARIS  SPLAT
  WARREN  TUPELO
SPIRITS  TELLSON
NOTIME  ABATE
OLA  MRSMALAPROP
OIL  ERROR  NIOBE
POL  REARS  SETIN
```

## 37

```
THIS  SLOGS  LAZE
REVIEWABLE  IRIS
ORANGEPEEL  BINS
DEN  RAISE  PEACE
     PERSE  BAR
RECESS  CENTRAL
ALIAS  FOOD  YULE
NARC  BOWLS  BRIG
ITCH  AREA  LEAVE
SEABIRD  CALLER
    RMN  GNARL
SCRAP  RAINY  ANA
OLIN  COTTONSWAB
LAND  OVEREXPOSE
EDDY  PESOS  ALAS
```

## 38

```
AESOP  PENAL  TET
BLISS  AMORE  AVE
NOTHINGISSO  KIN
EPEE  EERIE  BELT
RESALE  ENROL
   ADMIRABLEIN
DEFENSED  LIGATE
ELUL  REA  EVES
PILLAR  ASPIRERS
POLITICSASA
   TOOTH  ANGERS
BAIT  COBOL  AREA
OHM  SHORTMEMORY
USE  RISER  SUDAN
TOR  SEETO  STENO
```

## 39

```
OGLE  ANDS  MATES
PIER  DEEP  AROMA
ELSE  HULA  SLUMS
CATCHERINTHERYE
    TARO  YIN
PET  VENTURE  LOT
ALONE  ORO  FETE
SOWONESWILDOATS
SPEW  RUE  RESET
EEL  PAPRIKA  TRY
    IRS  TINS
JIMMIECRACKCORN
ADOBE  HULK  OBEY
VENUS  EDIE  RODE
ASSET  WEAR  NEST
```

## 40

```
ORCA  CCCP  OPALS
MEAD  REAL  ARIOT
ANIL  USNA  TODAY
RENAISSANCEMAN
    INON  ORO
HOE  DEACONS  MPG
ENNUI  RIG  SOAR
LEONARDODAVINCI
GALE  ONA  OCTET
ALA  PLATEAU  ERS
    CAL  DECA
  DANTEALIGHIERI
RICOH  LUBE  SYST
ERATO  UCLA  LEVI
CEDES  MIEN  ESPN
```

## 41

```
A B C S   C A M U S   F L O P
K O L A   A M A T I   L O V E
A M E N   S A L A D   A S E A
  B O C K I N T H E U S S R
      T I N A     A S H
E L N I N O   P E R U   E S S
N E A T     K A R M A   L E T
D A V Y J O N E S S L A G E R
U S A   A R I S E     R A T E
E E L   N A T E   F U R R O W
    J E T     G A G A
  A L E T O T H E C H I E F
Q U I T   R I A N T   G R A Y
E T T E   I N T R O   N I L E
D O E R   O T H E R   S E A T
```

## 42

```
B A S S   U N D O   W A L D O
O P A L   P A R S   A M O U R
U S M A R S H A L   R A N E E
T E E P E E   B O O T H I L L
      A T V     S I S
S C A L D   I B E A M   P S T
A R R A Y   D O D G E C I T Y
L O O M   S E R G E   A T O P
T O M B S T O N E   D R A K E
S K A   T A S E R   E S S E S
      M A I     S O B
O K C O R R A L   T I L D E S
I N A P T   W Y A T T E A R P
L E V E L   E R T E   E Z R A
S W E D E   S E E R   R E S T
```

## 43

```
P U M P   C A R A T   P A R A
S T A R   O V A T E   E X I T
S A R I   R E C O N   S L O E
T H E S T O C K M A R K E T
    M O N     N A Y
O B I   F E D   A C T   B A A
C O M P U T E R S Y S T E M S
C O M A   P O I     W E B S
U N I N V I T E D P E O P L E
R E X   A S H   E A R   S E T
    F R O     R I B
  T H E Y M I G H T C R A S H
S H O T   E D W I N   A U T O
I O W A   R E E V E   G R E G
N U L L   S A N E R   S A W S
```

## 44

```
M O W S   A G A P E   M E S H
E C H O   S H R E D   A U T O
S H O O T H O O P S   C L E O
A S O N E   S M U   A H E A D
    P E N   T A P E W O R M S
F A I R E R     G E M
I T T   T U B I N G   A L A S
S M U T   F O C U S   N A S H
H O P I   F L Y B O Y   N E A
    P A L   N A S D A Q
S N A P B E A N S   C C S
L I B Y A   F O E   H A L O S
E X I T   F I L M S T R I P S
D O D O   A R T I E   A D I N
S N E E   R E E S E   B E E S
```

## 45

```
C E L L O   C B E R   M A L E
O R I O N   H O N E   A L I T
C O F F E E A N D D A N I S H
A S E T   T I E   O R I O L E
      F U R   C L E A N E R
T A I P E I   A L E S
A S S E T   A S I N   S E N T
M E A T A N D P O T A T O E S
P A Y S   A D E S   H E N N A
      A M E N   D O W S E R
C R A M M E R   H E Y
A E R I A L   D O E   F R E E
P E A C H E S A N D C R E A M
E L B A   S I D E   H O I S T
S S S S   S T A Y   A G N E S
```

# 46

```
S C U F F ■ S C O T ■ S L O G
C A V I L ■ N A N A ■ T A L L
A R E T E ■ A R M S ■ E R M A
G R A Z E G R A Y S ■ A V E R
■ ■ ■ C A L C ■ E N L A C E
R O M P E R ■ A R L E S ■ ■
A X E L ■ D E S I ■ A T R I A
G E T A W A Y ■ S C R E A M S
A N Z I O ■ R E E L ■ E V A S
■ ■ N O M E N ■ E N L I S T
H O O P L A ■ T A R E ■ ■
E L A L ■ C H E C K C Z E C H
R I T A ■ R I R E ■ T I T H E
O V E N ■ O V E R ■ A N N U M
D A N E ■ S E R B ■ R E A M S
```

# 47

```
R A B A T ■ N E S T ■ D I M E
I R A N I ■ A X L E ■ E T A L
P I E T A ■ R I O T ■ L A R A
■ D I R E C T O R B I L L Y
T O E C A P ■ P A R ■ I O N
E L K ■ S O R T S ■ I N A N E
A G E D ■ C O O ■ C E O ■
M A R A T H O N E R F R A N K
■ D O S ■ T E A ■ A L E E
J A B O T ■ S O L T I ■ L A G
A M O ■ E R A ■ E N T E R S
N E W S M A N M O R L E Y ■
G L E E ■ I D O L ■ E R O D E
L I R A ■ S A R A ■ T R O O P
E A S T ■ E L O N ■ S E P T A
```

# 48

```
U S M A ■ E R R E D ■ T A L C
G O I N ■ L E A V E ■ O W E S
H U N D R E D Y A R D D A S H
■ N I E C E S ■ A O R T A
J O E ■ S T E ■ R I M ■ D A R
A F L A C ■ M O U R N ■ S T P
W A L N U T ■ S T A Y S ■
■ N I N E I N C H N A I L S ■
■ A P N E A ■ I N T A K E
L A S ■ L E A R N ■ K E V I N
O A T ■ A S P ■ O D E ■ A P E
A C O R N ■ U N R E A L ■
T H R E E M I L E I S L A N D
H E E D ■ D O N E E ■ O M N I
E N D S ■ S C A D S ■ E P E E
```

# 49

```
E G B D F ■ F O A M ■ V A M P
L A N A I ■ E L L A ■ E T U I
B R A W N ■ L A M A ■ N A S A
A B I G A I L V A N B U R E N
■ ■ L O S ■ D O S I D O
A T M O S T ■ U M P S ■ ■
C H I P ■ A N N L A N D E R S
C A D E T ■ O I L ■ S A M O A
T W I N S I S T E R ■ M I L L
■ ■ K N E E ■ O M E L E T
H O T T E A ■ B S A ■ ■
I N E E D S O M E A D V I C E
P I P E ■ N O O N ■ C I D E R
P O E M ■ I Z O D ■ A L O N G
O N E S ■ T E N S ■ P E L T S
```

# 50

```
M A S S ■ F A T E ■ C O A S T
C R O C ■ A D I N ■ U N D E R
S M A R T B O M B ■ R E L A Y
■ P A H ■ E L A L ■ A T O
■ P O P U L A R O P I N I O N
G A P E D A T ■ C O C O ■ ■
I C E S ■ L I P ■ U S H E R
G E R ■ H O T C A K E ■ A B E
I D A H O ■ S P A ■ T R O D
■ A M I E ■ O N E I D A S
H I P R E P L A C E M E N T ■
A V A ■ F O A M ■ M I O ■
R A R E R ■ I N T R A N S I T
S N I D E ■ N O L A ■ T E R I
H A S T E ■ E T C H ■ O D E S
```

## 51

| E | L | F | | | P | O | S | T | S | | P | E | O | N | S |
| L | I | E | | | O | N | T | O | P | | A | L | P | H | A |
| I | N | N | | | S | C | A | L | E | | S | M | E | L | L |
| J | A | C | K | I | E | G | L | E | A | S | O | N | | | |
| A | G | E | N | T | | | | C | U | E | | D | O | G | |
| H | E | R | O | | | P | A | T | H | S | | D | A | M | E |
| | | | W | E | I | G | H | | | F | E | T | A | L | |
| T | H | E | H | O | N | E | Y | M | O | O | N | E | R | S | |
| S | O | L | O | N | | | M | A | C | R | O | | | | |
| A | N | E | W | | E | R | E | C | T | | T | A | N | G | |
| R | E | V | | | I | R | E | | | M | E | T | O | O | |
| | | A | U | D | R | E | Y | M | E | A | D | O | W | S | |
| M | E | T | R | E | | S | W | I | R | L | | N | I | P | |
| O | M | E | G | A | | E | C | L | A | T | | E | S | E | |
| B | U | S | E | S | | S | A | L | S | A | | D | E | L | |

## 52

| I | N | T | E | R | | T | I | L | | G | U | S | T | O |
| S | A | U | D | I | | U | N | I | | A | S | P | E | R |
| M | I | L | I | T | A | N | T | S | | N | O | R | S | E |
| | F | I | T | Z | G | E | R | A | L | D | | I | T | S |
| | S | P | O | I | L | S | | A | H | I | T | | | |
| | | R | E | O | | H | O | W | I | T | Z | E | R | |
| H | A | D | | S | W | O | O | N | | T | E | T | E | |
| A | T | I | L | T | | W | O | E | | G | O | R | E | D |
| R | A | T | A | | E | D | S | E | L | | S | S | S | |
| I | T | Z | W | O | R | D | S | | M | I | R | | | |
| | I | N | R | E | | B | I | T | E | R | S | | | |
| S | U | N | | B | A | R | M | I | T | Z | V | A | H | |
| T | R | E | V | I | | T | E | N | S | I | O | N | A | L |
| A | S | S | E | T | | E | R | E | | E | K | I | N | G |
| B | A | S | E | S | | S | E | T | | R | E | N | E | E |

## 53

| S | C | R | I | P | | B | A | S | H | | L | A | D | Y |
| H | A | I | K | U | | A | N | T | E | | O | L | E | O |
| I | N | D | E | P | E | N | D | E | N | C | E | D | A | Y |
| N | E | E | | I | Q | S | | P | R | O | B | O | N | O |
| | | F | L | U | | G | O | I | N | | | | | |
| T | A | P | A | | I | R | O | N | | J | A | F | F | E |
| O | L | E | S | | N | I | L | | L | O | R | E | A | L |
| S | T | A | T | U | E | O | F | L | I | B | E | R | T | Y |
| C | E | L | E | B | S | | P | E | P | | T | R | E | S |
| A | R | E | N | A | | T | R | I | S | | H | Y | D | E |
| | | | N | E | R | O | | Y | M | A | | | | |
| A | T | I | N | G | L | E | | A | N | A | | E | E | L |
| J | U | L | Y | I | V | M | D | C | C | L | X | X | V | I |
| A | B | L | E | | I | O | N | E | | T | E | P | E | E |
| R | E | S | T | | S | R | A | S | | A | D | O | R | N |

## 54

| S | C | A | M | | A | R | A | B | | C | R | E | A | M |
| D | A | R | E | | D | A | L | E | | H | A | L | L | E |
| S | L | A | G | | R | I | L | E | | A | B | B | E | S |
| | F | L | A | T | O | N | O | N | E | S | B | A | C | H |
| | | W | H | I | S | T | | L | E | I | | | | |
| D | E | P | A | R | T | | P | A | S | T | I | M | E | |
| E | L | A | T | E | | E | R | I | N | | B | U | N | |
| M | O | S | T | W | A | N | T | E | D | L | I | S | Z | T |
| O | P | T | | L | I | E | D | | A | N | E | A | R | |
| S | E | E | S | R | E | D | | S | P | U | N | K | Y | |
| | | A | I | R | | C | O | L | I | N | | | | |
| T | O | O | H | O | T | T | O | H | A | N | D | E | L | |
| E | C | L | A | T | | O | L | A | V | | A | T | O | Z |
| S | H | A | R | E | | M | O | R | E | | T | A | L | E |
| S | O | N | A | R | | E | R | A | S | | E | L | A | N |

## 55

| D | O | I | N | | E | V | I | T | A | | E | G | A | D |
| A | R | C | O | | M | A | C | E | S | | B | E | D | E |
| H | E | A | R | T | B | R | E | A | K | H | O | T | E | L |
| L | O | N | G | H | A | I | R | | | A | L | O | N | E |
| | | T | E | R | S | E | | S | E | R | I | F | | |
| A | S | H | | E | S | S | E | N | C | E | | F | A | T |
| D | E | E | J | A | Y | | X | O | O | | M | O | N | O |
| O | G | L | E | D | | H | U | B | | O | R | F | E | O |
| R | A | P | T | | P | A | R | | B | U | S | M | A | N |
| E | L | M | | D | E | L | B | E | R | T | | Y | R | S |
| | | Y | M | C | A | S | | L | I | L | A | C | | |
| A | S | S | A | I | | D | I | S | A | L | L | O | W | |
| W | H | E | N | I | M | S | I | X | T | Y | F | O | U | R |
| E | E | L | S | | D | E | V | I | L | | R | U | S | E |
| S | A | F | E | | S | C | A | R | Y | | E | D | E | N |

## 56

```
J A I L   M E T A L   D A Z E
U N T O   A D O R E   E R O S
S T I R   C I R C A   L O O T
T E N D E R F O O T   T A M E
      L O Y     H O A R S E
B O W M A N   F L E A
A L I E N   C O U R T Y A R D
L A L A   T A C K Y   A L A R
I V Y L E A G U E   B R A K E
      P I E S   C O N N E D
S Q U E A L     L A O
A U N T   W A T E R M E T E R
B A T H   I R A T E   M A X I
O K I E   N I C H E   I R I S
T E L L   D A T E R   T A T E
```

## 57

```
L O P   F L A S H   A T L A S
E R A   E E R I E   D U A N E
A C U   D A R L A   E L I T E
H A L T   R A L P H N A D E R
    R A I N Y     I O N
S M E L T S   V A R I E T Y
W A V E S   F A X E D   H E F
A C E S   E R R E D   R E A L
P A R   A V A I L   T E R S E
    W E L D I N G   D O N A T E
        E A T   T O M E I
J O H N M A D D E N   E D A M
A R E N A   I R A N I   E W E
B A R O N   N O S E D   R A N
S L A N T   O P E R A   S Y D
```

## 58

```
P A M P A S   S T E W   P T A
E T E R N E   C O D E   E A R
N O N O N A N E T T E   P R E
S M U T   M O N O   V E E P S
    E L A T E   G I L L
A M B I E N T   S A L I E N T
D U A N E   A T I T   A M E S
I N B   K I K I D E E   O V A
N C A A   D E L E   A S K E R
S H A R P E N   S A V I O R S
    U N I S   A L I E N
S T R O P   O B I S   A I D A
A A H   P U P U P L A T T E R
L I U   I R E S   E R R A N T
E L M   N I N E   S C A N T Y
```

## 59

```
B L D G S   S S W   A T W A R
L E E R S   C H I   R H I N E
A T L A S   R E D G I A N T S
S H U N   O A R E D   N E H I
T A X D O D G E R S   B I Z
S L E E V E     S C A L E
    U L C E R   E A R L S
    H E L L S A N G E L S
C L O V E   A T A R I
H I R E S     O N S I T E
A S S   S T R A I G H T A S
U S E S   T O E I N   E A R P
C O M P A D R E S   W I L M A
E M A I L   M D L   E L I A N
R E N T S   E Y E   D A C C A
```

## 60

```
S T A N   A G O G   D A M E S
H I T E   D U N E   A L A M O
O N E A   M A T T   L Y S O L
W E A T H E R V A N E   E T O
M A S   I N D   L O Y   R I M
E R E C T   S N I T   T A C O
    H O B   O F A   I T O N
    I N A N O T H E R V E I N
D C O N   R H O   Y A T
R E S T   N E W S   S O L O S
A W E   R E B   P A C   E R E
C A R   Y O U R E S O V A I N
U T I C A   R E E K   I D E A
L E N I N   B I D E   V E N T
A R G O S   S N O W   A N T E
```

## 71

| D | O | R | S | A | | F | L | O | R | A | | I | D | S |
| I | R | O | N | S | | L | O | C | A | L | | T | E | L |
| A | B | O | O | K | M | U | S | T | B | E | | S | L | A |
| | | F | R | A | M | E | | | E | X | P | E | R | T |
| M | A | T | T | | E | N | C | L | | | I | L | I | E |
| A | L | O | E | S | | T | H | E | A | X | E | F | O | R |
| I | M | P | R | O | V | | E | N | T | E | R | | | |
| M | S | S | | N | E | G | A | T | O | R | | H | E | M |
| | | E | A | T | A | T | | M | O | D | E | N | A | |
| T | H | E | F | R | O | Z | E | N | | X | R | A | Y | S |
| W | E | L | T | | A | D | U | E | | E | R | A | T | |
| E | R | A | S | E | R | | A | N | G | S | T | | | |
| L | E | T | | S | E | A | I | N | S | I | D | E | U | S |
| V | I | E | | A | D | H | O | C | | G | E | N | T | S |
| E | N | D | | I | S | S | U | E | | I | N | S | E | T |

## 72

| U | K | E | S | | E | L | B | A | | A | C | T | E | D |
| N | O | A | H | | R | E | A | P | | L | A | R | V | A |
| C | A | R | Y | G | R | A | N | T | | B | R | E | E | D |
| A | L | L | | L | A | S | S | | W | I | R | E | R | S |
| P | A | Y | M | E | N | T | | M | A | N | Y | | | |
| | | | A | N | T | | S | A | Y | O | N | A | R | A |
| S | T | E | R | N | | S | H | I | N | | A | J | A | X |
| T | A | X | I | | A | M | A | Z | E | | T | A | K | E |
| A | R | I | A | | D | O | M | E | | T | I | R | E | D |
| B | A | T | H | M | A | T | S | | R | I | O | | | |
| | | | C | O | P | E | | S | E | A | N | C | E | S |
| A | G | H | A | S | T | | F | E | A | R | | A | V | A |
| F | L | A | R | E | | J | I | M | C | A | R | R | E | Y |
| R | I | L | E | Y | | E | D | I | T | | C | O | N | S |
| O | B | E | Y | S | | B | O | S | S | | A | L | T | O |

## 73

| M | U | R | A | L | | F | L | O | W | N | | J | A | M |
| A | C | U | R | A | | A | U | D | I | O | | A | G | O |
| S | L | I | M | P | I | C | K | E | N | S | | N | E | O |
| H | A | N | A | | R | T | E | | D | O | O | V | E | R |
| | | | N | I | A | | | G | U | A | V | A | | |
| | S | K | I | N | N | Y | D | I | P | P | I | N | G | |
| F | I | E | | T | I | A | R | A | S | | N | E | R | D |
| I | N | T | E | L | | C | E | N | | K | E | Y | I | N |
| R | E | T | D | | S | H | A | N | I | A | | C | P | A |
| | S | L | I | G | H | T | M | I | S | T | A | K | E | |
| | | E | T | H | O | S | | | A | O | L | | | |
| R | E | D | H | O | T | | A | D | A | | S | K | E | D |
| O | A | R | | S | P | A | R | E | C | H | A | N | G | E |
| D | R | U | | T | U | X | E | S | | O | C | E | A | N |
| E | L | M | | S | T | E | A | K | | N | E | E | D | Y |

## 74

| T | O | N | G | A | | S | O | S | | W | E | R | E | A |
| U | S | U | A | L | | A | N | N | | I | N | A | L | L |
| N | O | Z | Z | L | E | | Y | E | A | | D | A | Z | Z | L | E |
| A | L | L | E | G | R | O | | F | E | E | B | L | E | R |
| S | E | E | N | | E | N | D | U | P | | L | E | N | T |
| | | | A | S | T | A | R | | I | R | E | | | |
| T | H | E | S | A | U | R | I | | C | Y | S | T | I | C |
| A | I | D | | F | R | A | Z | Z | L | E | D | | O | D | O |
| R | E | D | D | E | N | | L | I | N | E | S | M | A | N |
| | | | U | S | E | | E | N | T | R | E | | | |
| D | O | S | E | | R | I | D | G | E | | S | P | A | M |
| E | V | I | L | E | S | T | | E | R | A | S | U | R | E |
| G | U | Z | Z | L | E | | E | R | R | | F | I | Z | Z | L | E |
| A | L | L | E | N | | M | O | E | | A | L | L | E | S |
| S | E | E | D | Y | | S | O | D | | R | E | E | S | E |

## 75

| B | R | O | W | | P | U | M | A | S | | H | A | S | P |
| L | O | N | E | | I | S | I | A | H | | Y | O | K | E |
| O | N | E | E | I | G | H | T | H | U | N | D | R | E | D |
| B | A | H | | N | E | E | T | | T | E | E | T | E | R |
| | | | A | S | T | O | R | | P | S | I | | A | T | O |
| C | A | N | T | O | N | | T | O | O | L | S | | | |
| E | N | D | A | T | | S | E | L | F | | C | O | K | E |
| O | N | E | T | O | U | C | H | O | F | V | E | N | U | S |
| S | A | D | E | | N | O | E | S | | I | N | E | R | T |
| | | | S | I | D | L | E | | A | S | T | U | T | E |
| M | I | A | | C | I | D | | C | R | I | S | P | | |
| A | N | T | H | E | M | | C | A | R | O | | P | E | A |
| O | N | E | A | R | M | E | D | B | A | N | D | I | T | S |
| R | E | A | D | | E | M | I | L | Y | | O | N | U | S |
| I | R | M | A | | D | O | V | E | S | | A | G | I | N |

# The New York Times

## Crossword Puzzles

### The #1 name in crosswords

Available at your local bookstore or online at nytimes.com/nytstore

### Coming Soon

| | | |
|---|---|---|
| Crossword Challenge | 0-312-33951-8 | $12.95/$18.95 Can. |
| Crosswords for a Rainy Day | 0-312-33952-6 | $6.95/$9.95 Can. |
| Crosswords for Stress Relief | 0-312-33953-4 | $6.95/$9.95 Can. |
| Crosswords to Beat the Clock | 0-312-33954-2 | $6.95/$9.95 Can. |
| Large-Print Will Shortz's Favorite Crosswords | 0-312-33959-3 | $10.95/$15.95 Can. |
| Daily Crosswords Vol. 69 | 0-312-33956-9 | $9.95/$14.95 Can. |
| Large-Print Big Book of Easy Crosswords | 0-312-33958-5 | $12.95/$18.95 Can. |
| Easy Crosswords Vol. 6 | 0-312-33957-7 | $10.95/$15.95 Can. |
| Will Shortz's Funniest Crosswords Vol. 2 | 0-312-33960-7 | $9.95/$14.95 Can. |

### Special Editions

| | | |
|---|---|---|
| Super Sunday Crosswords | 0-312-33115-0 | $10.95/$15.95 Can. |
| Will Shortz's Funniest Crosswords | 0-312-32489-8 | $9.95/$14.95 Can. |
| Will Shortz's Sunday Favorites | 0-312-32488-X | $9.95/$14.95 Can. |
| Crosswords for a Brain Workout | 0-312-32610-6 | $6.95/$9.95 Can. |
| Crosswords to Boost Your Brainpower | 0-312-32033-7 | $6.95/$9.95 Can. |
| Crossword All-Stars | 0-312-31004-8 | $9.95/$14.95 Can. |
| Will Shortz's Favorites | 0-312-30613-X | $9.95/$14.95 Can. |
| Bonus Crosswords | 0-312-31033-X | $9.95/$14.95 Can. |
| Ultimate Omnibus | 0-312-31622-4 | $6.95/$9.95 Can. |

### Daily Crosswords

| | | |
|---|---|---|
| Monday through Friday | 0-312-30058-1 | $9.95/$14.95 Can. |
| Daily Crosswords Vol. 68 | 0-312-33434-6 | $9.95/$14.95 Can. |
| Daily Crosswords Vol. 67 | 0-312-32437-5 | $9.95/$14.95 Can. |
| Daily Crosswords Vol. 66 | 0-312-32436-7 | $9.95/$14.95 Can. |
| Daily Crosswords Vol. 65 | 0-312-32034-5 | $9.95/$14.95 Can. |
| Daily Crosswords Vol. 64 | 0-312-31458-2 | $9.95/$14.95 Can. |
| Daily Crosswords Vol. 63 | 0-312-30947-3 | $9.95/$14.95 Can. |
| Daily Crosswords Vol. 62 | 0-312-30512-5 | $9.95/$14.95 Can. |
| Daily Crosswords Vol. 61 | 0-312-30057-3 | $9.95/$14.95 Can. |

### Easy Crosswords

| | | |
|---|---|---|
| Easy Crosswords Vol. 5 | 0-312-32438-3 | $9.95/$14.95 Can. |
| Easy Crosswords Vol. 4 | 0-312-30448-X | $9.95/$14.95 Can. |
| Easy Crosswords Vol. 3 | 0-312-28912-X | $9.95/$14.95 Can. |
| Easy Crosswords Vol. 2 | 0-312-28172-2 | $9.95/$14.95 Can. |

### Tough Crosswords

| | | |
|---|---|---|
| Tough Crosswords Vol. 12 | 0-312-32442-1 | $10.95/$15.95 Can. |
| Tough Crosswords Vol. 11 | 0-312-31456-6 | $10.95/$15.95 Can. |
| Tough Crosswords Vol. 10 | 0-312-30060-3 | $10.95/$15.95 |
| Tough Crosswords Vol. 9 | 0-312-28173-0 | $10.95/$15.95 Can. |

### Sunday Crosswords

| | | |
|---|---|---|
| Sunday Crosswords Vol. 30 | 0-312-33538-5 | $9.95/$14.95 Can. |
| Sunday Crosswords Vol. 29 | 0-312-32038-8 | $9.95/$14.95 Can. |
| Sunday Crosswords Vol. 28 | 0-312-30515-X | $9.95/$14.95 Can. |
| Sunday Crosswords Vol. 27 | 0-312-28414-4 | $9.95/$14.95 Can. |

### Large-Print Crosswords

| | | |
|---|---|---|
| Large-Print Big Book of Holiday Crosswords | 0-312-33092-8 | $12.95/$18.95 Can. |
| Large-Print Crosswords for Your Coffeebreak | 0-312-33109-6 | $10.95/$15.95 Can. |
| Large-Print Crosswords for a Brain Workout | 0-312-32612-2 | $10.95/$15.95 Can. |
| Large-Print Crosswords to Boost Your Brainpower | 0-312-32037-X | $11.95/$17.95 Can. |
| Large-Print Easy Omnibus | 0-312-32439-1 | $12.95/$18.95 Can. |
| Large-Print Daily Vol. 2 | 0-312-33111-8 | $10.95/$15.95 Can. |
| Large-Print Daily Crosswords | 0-312-31457-4 | $10.95/$15.95 Can. |
| Large-Print Omnibus Vol. 5 | 0-312-32036-1 | $12.95/$18.95 Can. |
| Large-Print Omnibus Vol. 4 | 0-312-30514-1 | $12.95/$18.95 Can. |
| Large-Print Omnibus Vol. 3 | 0-312-28441-1 | $12.95/$18.95 Can. |

### Omnibus

| | | |
|---|---|---|
| Big Book of Holiday Crosswords | 0-312-33533-4 | $11.95/$17.95 Can. |
| Crosswords for a Lazy Afternoon | 0-312-33108-8 | $11.95/$17.95 Can. |
| Tough Omnibus Vol. 1 | 0-312-32441-3 | $11.95/$14.95 Can. |
| Easy Omnibus Vol. 3 | 0-312-33537-7 | $11.95/$17.95 Can. |
| Easy Omnibus Vol. 2 | 0-312-32035-3 | $11.95/$17.95 Can. |
| Easy Omnibus Vol. 1 | 0-312-30513-3 | $11.95/$17.95 Can. |
| Daily Omnibus Vol. 14 | 0-312-33534-2 | $11.95/$17.95 Can. |
| Daily Omnibus Vol. 13 | 0-312-32031-0 | $11.95/$17.95 Can. |
| Daily Omnibus Vol. 12 | 0-312-30511-7 | $11.95/$17.95 Can. |
| Sunday Omnibus Vol. 8 | 0-312-32440-5 | $11.95/$17.95 Can. |
| Sunday Omnibus Vol. 7 | 0-312-30950-3 | $11.95/$17.95 Can. |
| Sunday Omnibus Vol. 6 | 0-312-28913-8 | $11.95/$17.95 Can. |

### Variety Puzzles

| | | |
|---|---|---|
| Acrostic Puzzles Vol. 9 | 0-312-30949-X | $9.95/$14.95 Can. |
| Sunday Variety Puzzles | 0-312-30059-X | $9.95/$14.95 Can. |

### Portable Size Format

| | | |
|---|---|---|
| Quick Crosswords | 0-312-33114-2 | $6.95/$9.95 Can. |
| More Sun, Sand and Crosswords | 0-312-33112-6 | $6.95/$9.95 Can. |
| Planes, Trains and Crosswords | 0-312-33113-4 | $6.95/$9.95 Can. |
| Cup of Tea and Crosswords | 0-312-32435-9 | $6.95/$9.95 Can. |
| Crosswords for Your Bedside | 0-312-32032-9 | $6.95/$9.95 Can. |
| Beach Bag Crosswords | 0-312-31455-8 | $6.95/$9.95 Can. |
| Crosswords for the Work Week | 0-312-30952-X | $6.95/$9.95 Can. |
| T.G.I.F. Crosswords | 0-312-33116-9 | $6.95/$9.95 Can. |
| Super Saturday | 0-312-30604-0 | $6.95/$9.95 Can. |
| Sun, Sand and Crosswords | 0-312-30076-X | $6.95/$9.95 Can. |
| Crosswords to Exercise Your Brain | 0-312-33536-9 | $6.95/$9.95 Can. |
| Crosswords for Your Breakfast Table | 0-312-33535-0 | $6.95/$9.95 Can. |

### For Young Solvers

| | | |
|---|---|---|
| New York Times on the Web Crosswords for Teens | 0-312-28911-1 | $6.95/$9.95 Can. |
| Outrageous Crossword Puzzles and Word Games for Kids | 0-312-28915-1 | $6.95/$9.95 Can. |
| More Outrageous Crossword Puzzles for Kids | 0-312-30062-X | $6.95/$9.95 Can. |

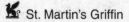 St. Martin's Griffin